T0368208

Hispanic Women Seeking Higher Leadership Roles in Business

Hispanic Women Seeking Higher Leadership Roles in Business

Sylvia C. Motta, PhD

To order additional copies of this book, contact:
Xlibris Corporation
1-888-795-4274
www.Xlibris.com
Orders@Xlibris.com
87253

Contents

Introduction...7

Chapter 1 History of Mentoring 19

Chapter 2 Hispanic women in Today's Workforce:
What does this mean?...32

Chapter 3 Organizational Responsibility.............................45

Leadership in the workforce 51
Importance of mentoring in an organization 56
Mentoring programs in the business world today 62

Chapter 4 Impact on Hispanic Women...............................67

Chapter 5 Future Implications for the Hispanic
Woman in the Workplace 82

Bibliography..93

Introduction

Looking back, I think I have always been passionate about the advancement of minority women in the workforce. I think it began from watching my mother work long, physical hours at the local factory in Chelsea, Massachusetts. She bought a house back in the mid 1970's across from the factory so she could get home quicker to her family. I remember watching her walking up the hill from Highland Park covered in dust and weary looking. She would get home, give all of us six kids a kiss, shower, and lay down for an hour because she was so exhausted.

My mother did this for 21 years until the company moved out of Chelsea. I remember feeling a little relieved that the company eventually relocated out of Chelsea only because of the physical toll it took on my mom. I used to ask her why she worked in a job that made her so tired and she would reply, "Mija, the pay is good and they have good benefits." It left me wondering why a woman who I considered to be the smartest woman in the world would subject herself to such physical labor.

Over the years, I slowly began to understand why my mother worked so hard in a dead end job. I also learned how to become a dedicated, hard working, committed employee because of my mother. My mother worked for five major companies in the span of 40 years in the United States. Most of us have had that many jobs by the time we reach 20. These jobs paid minimum wage, required long hours, and had no room for advancement especially for women who had little education and an accent. My mother has been an American citizen since 1977 and highly intelligent but too many biases existed during this period for a female, much less a female from El Salvador, to get ahead in the workforce.

Yet this strong woman managed to work hard enough to buy a home, raise six children in a loving atmosphere, take care of a sick husband, and pay the bills in a timely manner. Without realizing it, my mother was teaching her only daughter an awareness of the role of women as head of household and in the workforce. Specifically, she made me aware of the difficult role of a minority woman in the workforce and how difficult it is for a Hispanic woman to balance home and work.

Watching my mother over the years naturally taught me to be a loyal, dedicated worker. As a teenager, one of my first jobs was working in the kitchen department at a hospital in Boston. I worked at this job for five years and it was a very demanding, physical job. I left this job while attending my second year in college and expecting my first child. I do not quite recall why I left the job but felt it was time to move. The job had become too mundane and somewhat of a dead end for me. I also did not want to risk getting hurt while I was pregnant due to the physical nature of the job and wet floors.

My next job was working with the U.S. Census collecting data in my neighborhood. I loved this job because it brought me in contact with people living in Chelsea and East Boston and gathering information based on their income, family size, employment history, education, etc. Most of the people I encountered were Hispanics with similar upbringing as me. I think this is why they were very open with their responses or else they felt bad for a seven month pregnant woman walking around in the sweltering summer months! Most interesting about this job was seeing how many Hispanic women were in the workforce and noticing their income bracket which was in the very low end. They were also working mothers.

It was very nice meeting people who lived in my neighborhood and discovering what they did for a living. I met many hard working families who opened their doors to me and did not mind me asking them a lot of personal questions. I think it was the first time I realized that despite my city's high poverty rate there were a lot of people working but struggling to make ends meet. It became an eye opening period for me. I realized the importance of an education and finding a job that would enable me to be financially secure especially where I was beginning to start a family.

It was during this time in the early 1990's that I began to work for an organization that would impact my life, beliefs, and become part of the reason of why I decided to write this book. I wrote this book to inspire women, especially Hispanics, that while there will be many obstacles to overcome in the professional working world and simultaneously having a family with persistence, education, and determination it will pay off. It may not be the path that you initially planned but in the end, most of us will have learned what is most important to us and what will make us happy. I learned the hard way but ultimately I became a much stronger and independent woman.

I have come to the conclusion that in my life I found a lot of things that what I expected, demanded, and gave in my personal life was something I also expected in my professional career. Some of those things were commitment, trust, recognition, guidance, and mentoring. As a woman, when I did not receive this in my relationship things began to fall apart. The same thing happened in the workplace. Much like personal relationships, when attention begins to lag, commitment flies out the door, and appreciation and recognition is not given, women will react. You have two choices and those choices are you either give up or you fight for what you want and deserve. Most of us Hispanic women today will fight for what we believe we have worked very hard in our life. Of course this is not different from what most people believe but the difference is that as Hispanic women we have faced difficulties in both our personal and professional lives due to biases from both the society we live in and the culture we were born into. In the past, we had to give up our attempts at having a professional career or furthering our education but this is no longer true. We now have choices and independence to stand behind what we believe in that makes us happy.

Today's fastest growing workforce consists of educated, Hispanic women who mostly have dual responsibilities. They work and they are head of households. They have children and work full-time. They pursue and education and are responsible for taking care of the family. They seek a professional career but also support their husbands' careers. How does a minority woman in today's workforce overcome advancement obstacles while still maintaining their responsibilities at home because of persistent biases that exist in the workforce for minority women?

One such way, I firmly believe, Hispanic women can advance into leadership positions are by having mentors in the workplace. As Hispanic women, most of us have had a mentor in our homes. For example, my greatest mentor has been my mother. Through her, I have learned lessons and lived experiences that even Harvard Business School would envy. While business schools have created fancy names for leadership styles such as transactional or transformational my mom taught me simply. She minced no words when it came to providing direction and guidance but in addition, provided a lot of feeling, understanding, and explanations. It was not until later that I realized she had taught me the fundamentals in transactional and transformational leadership and how to use both simultaneously. Needlessly, I grew up knowing how to use these leadership styles effortlessly. Her compassion also provided me with the ability to understand how important empathy is when communicating with your workforce. It is why I believe mentoring is so vital to a minority women's growth in an organization.

Mentoring partnerships in organizations help minority women advance into senior leadership positions. Discovering and learning to overcome the underlying causes of resistance and eliminating organizational barriers to mentoring programs is important in understanding if such problems are hindering minority women's paths to senior leadership positions. Mentoring has played a major role in helping individuals achieve career advancements and professional development. With today's workforce facing a greater number of women seeking management positions, organizations must look at ways in which to improve the ways in which women can attain these positions. Historically, most mentors have been white males in senior positions within the company. Over time, organizations have benefited from having a greater variety of role models. The representation of role models which include women and minorities is still low. As the number of people who enter the workforce declines but the number of women workers increases, organizations must increase opportunities for women to have upward career growth.

The interesting thing about minority women in the workforce is that minority women today are educated and have experience working in their fields. Many women may have begun with an entry level position and with experience gained skills that have led them to seek upward mobility. Most women today have pursued a degree in their chosen field while holding down a job. Some women have also raised a family while holding down a job and attending school. This makes them unique because compared to most of their male counterparts, minority women are multitasking. Minority women are intertwining both their personal and professional lives. This is difficult to do but it is being done by women. Unfortunately or fortunately depending on which way you look at it, minority women took on these challenges based on the goals they placed as to what they wanted to accomplish in their lives. Many women are raising children as single parents and have decided that instead of depending on a system to take care of them like in the past, many minority women instead chose to get an education and enter the workforce. In addition, changes were taken place in the welfare system which forced many women to enter the workforce. The Personal Responsibility and Work Opportunity Reconciliation Act (PRWORA) became law in 1996 that required shifting poor women off welfare and into the workforce.

At the same time, businesses were recognizing the need to attract and retain female talent due to changing demographics (Robinson & Dechant, 1997). Unfortunately, the rate of advancement for minorities has not equaled their increased educational achievements and career opportunities (Gathers, 2003; Ruderman & Ohlott, 1995; Thomas, 2001). In the U.S., the Catalyst Census released a report that showed the glass ceiling is still firmly in place (Catalyst, 2005a). Glass ceiling has been defined as "a barrier inhibiting the advancement of women to higher executive positions" (Gregory, 2002, p.62). The Catalyst Census report revealed that 50.3% of all management and professional positions were held by women yet only 7.9% of Fortune 500 top earners and 1.4% of Fortune 500 CEO's were women. The Catalyst study exposed how gender-based stereotyping sabotaged women in the workplace. Another Catalyst report revealed that there continued to be severe under-representation of women and minorities on corporate boards of the Fortune 100 when compared to general U.S. population demographics for race and gender (Catalyst, 2005b). A particular area of concern included the lack of representation of minority women. Women continue to be underrepresented in top leadership positions but overrepresented in bottom entry level positions.

Many organizations recognize diversity is a business issue (Mannix & Neale, 2005). When glass ceilings existed, organizations were not valuing women and minorities (Powell & Butterfield, 2002). Organization's attempted to eliminate their glass ceiling by attempting efforts at initiating diversity management programs (Athey, Avery, & Zemsky, 2000). Organizations faced difficulties because of the failure to recognize the importance of valuing individual talent and not because they were a member of a special group (Ingham, 2006). At this point, leadership began to play a major role in making a difference. Recognition that diversity was a business imperative, acknowledgement of the benefits of diversity, and having people personally committed were identified as the human factors in assisting with the success of diversity initiatives (Wentling, 2004). A diversified workforce allowed managers to make better decisions, cultivate new ideas, increased market share to an increasingly diverse customer base, and helped improve the agility and adaptability of the organization (Allen & Montgomery, 2001). Despite recognizing the benefits of having a diversified workforce, organizations still failed with their diversity initiatives because organizations struggle in understanding individuals who have different values and language skills. In recent years, organizations have attempted to create formal mentoring programs which have top leadership support, careful selection of mentors and mentees, and training programs on expectations concerning mentoring relationships (Joiner, Bartram & Garreffa, 2004). As Gregory (2002) noted about minority women and glass ceiling, "From beneath such a barrier, they cannot learn by observing those working above it, and in addition, they are isolated from and invisible to corporate decision makers" p.62

The sad part of being a minority women in today's workforce is facing the fact that barriers still exist and how frustrating and exhausting it can be to women to overcome. Organizations may insist and adamantly demonstrate that they have systems and programs in place that may appear to be wonderful and sensational but dig deep enough and not everything appears to be rosy. In my experience, I have witnessed and lived through enough experiences to know this so called glass ceiling is very firmly in place. Most certainly women have advanced into leadership positions but look closely and those women are just an iota of the community they serve or the customers that are buying their products.

Even more sadly is acknowledging a "glass ceiling" still exists in the 21st century despite the creation of the Equal Pay Act of 1963 which required men and women be given equal pay for equal work in the same organization and I would like to add an opportunity at promotions. Often times, women have been placed in a situation that makes it hard to balance home and work responsibilities. A series of emotions and a sense of guilt often come into play for these women. Furthermore, when women educated Hispanic women are placed in a position of leadership they are then placed in a situation where they must prove themselves and are placed under a microscope where they must be under scrutiny and criticism that male counterparts did not appear to have to similarly encounter. This scrutiny is unfair because Hispanic women have not been given the support and guidance to often handle situation they have not had prior experience due to lack of exposure and preparedness contingent to their male counterparts. While some businesses have made changes and begun to show some interest in diversifying their senior leadership line there still is huge amounts of improvement and efforts needed to make and prove it is happening.

Because these efforts are sometimes happening it has now become a reason white males believe they are losing competitive advantage, opportunity, and overall control of the workplace as a result of the inclusion of women and minorities. In their work, Ryan and Haslam (2007) found that women who break through the glass ceiling must then face a "glass cliff" where they are at risk of even more failure. The Glass Cliff means when women are chosen for leadership positions when the risk of failure is very high. It is an impossible task that sets women up for failure and often has a male waiting in the background ready to sweep in and save the day. In my previous experience this has often been the case. I was often given positions where I basically did clean up and faced the blunt of backlash. With limited resources and support, I often faired better than most in my outcomes. I was successful in implementing new processes but I also was not the most popular and well-liked person. I do believe I earned the respect of some people but not the right people. By this I mean the people who could help advance my career.

Does this lack of recognition and support ever end? Unfortunately, the answer is not yet but it does not mean it is impossible. Here is where Hispanic women, I believe, have an advantage. It is a new era where things have drastically changed for the educated Hispanic woman seeking professional growth. The Hispanic woman has made changes and adjustments in her personal life that allow her to be a dominant force in today's workforce.

The advantage begins with recognizing the importance of having a positive role model who ends up being your mentor. I have been fortunate enough to have had such a person in my life. My role model/mentor is, Edith Motta, my mother. I strongly believe it takes someone who knows you the best and is a part of your life, boosts your motivation, encourages, supports, and yet gives you honest feedback who makes a difference. My mom is a sensational role model and I am still in awe at what she managed to accomplish and I only hope to mimic. I count my blessings at how fortunate I am to have a strong, intelligent, witty woman as my mother for a role model and mentor. Because of my mother, I became determined to be one for my own children and the community I serve.

As a result, I began my professional journey as a willing receptor to learn as much as I could from those who became a part of my professional world and have known in my personal life. I would like to put special emphasis on my personal acquaintances. I have been fortunate (and this was also because of my mother) to have grown up in a close-knit neighborhood and am proud to acknowledge that many of my childhood friends continue to be my friends. Most especially, a core of women who have grown to be absolutely wonderful accomplished, successful women in both their personal and professional lives. Because of our deep and bonding relationship, they have influenced the woman I am today. I took almost every piece of advice, compliment, and words of encouragement, support, and criticism and viewed them as opportunities for growth. At the same time, I supplemented this journey with an education. The blending of work and home experience and educational development became my launching pad at chipping away at this so called glass ceiling.

I also want to address the term I identify myself with and one I use throughout this book and that is the term Hispanic. While in England, I was part of a discussion with two of my friends regarding the terms Hispanic versus Latino. According to U.S. Census Bureau, the term Hispanic defines a region of origin not a person's race. The U.S. Census Bureau used the term to describe any person, regardless of race, creed, or color whose origins are Mexican, Puerto Rican, Cuban, Central or South American, or of some other Hispanic origin (retrieved from *http://factfinder. census.gov*). The term Hispanic is associated with areas conquered by the Spaniards called Hispaniola. Hispanic describes cultures or countries that were once under Spanish rule. Latino refers to countries that were once under Roman rule. These countries included Italy, France, Spain, etc. Furthermore, there has been a general consensus that older generations prefer the term Latino while the younger generations prefer the term Hispanic. Yet, others prefer to describe themselves by the country of origin but in general most people prefer the term Hispanic.

In this book, I will continue to discuss some of the advantages and disadvantages Hispanic women have in today's workforce. I will also review the history of mentoring and the creation of laws to protect minorities in the workplace. I will also write about organizational responsibility in creating successful mentoring programs and the importance of mentoring in the workplace, and the impact it has had on Hispanic women. Lastly, I will discuss future implications for the Hispanic woman in the workplace.

Chapter 1

History of Mentoring

Historically, mentoring can be traced back to Greek mythology (Moberg & Velasquez, 2004; Sosik & Lee, 2002). In the *Odyssey*, Mentor, disguised as the Greek Goddess Athena, was a close friend of Odysseus who closely protected, nurtured, and guided Odysseus' son, Telemachus, into a strong leader and protector of his land and home. Similarly, in business, mentoring was an informal process in which men who had been with the organization for a long time helped younger, potentially talented men successfully transition into their new roles and helped them understand and adapt to the organization's culture (Wasburn & Crespo, 2006). Unlike the Odyssey, though, most mentors were not women mentoring young men. In the U.S., white European, physically fit, heterosexual men have traditionally defined the workplace norms and standards by which all others have been judged (Agocs & Burr, 1996; Blank & Slipp, 1994). The existence of an old boys' network usually excluded minorities from taking part and made them feel like outsiders (Schuck & Liddle, 2004). This old boys' network behavior typically associated itself with what was believed to be strictly masculine traits such as aggressiveness, competitiveness, independence, and authority (Clugson et al., 2000; Meyerson & Fletcher, 2000; Van Vianen & Fischer, 2002).

In addition, most organization's mentors were predominantly white males so historically mentors were likely to select mentees perceived to be similar (Thomas, 1990). These white males tended to have an education, come from a middle-class home, and held professional jobs. They would then be mentored by a senior level executive who introduced and exposed them to the organization's culture and norms. These senior level executives usually consisted of older men who were preparing for retirement and ready to pass their knowledge onto someone who reminded them of their younger self. These senior level executives held high performing operation positions with experience in optimizing organizational processes and would pass their knowledge onto their young, male mentees. These young white males were then groomed to pretty much run business much like their former predecessors and they in turn would mentor new mentees who also reminded them of themselves, etc. Traditionally, men were taking care of business at work and women were taking care of business at home. This pattern of existence was the norm for a time in the United States.

Subtle changes began to happen in the world that caused these dynamics to slowly begin to change in the United States. I attribute some of these changes to more women entering the labor force after World War II causing women to find jobs to support their families while men were off fighting in the war. Women began to earn their own money for the first time and they liked the financial independence it gave them. Many of them also had a family to care for without the support of their husbands. Last but not least, women were learning to understand the responsibility of being head of household and the responsibilities associated in this role. Women have always been in charge of household responsibilities but in the past needed the financial support of their husbands to manage and this changed when women entered the workforce. Women now were the breadwinners who became solely responsible for keeping their family financially afloat while their husbands were overseas. When the war ended, many women remained in the workforce. Some of them liked the feeling of socialization and new friendships and bonding that happened outside the home. They valued making new friends and acquaintances at work which never happened at home.

Another factor that affected the reasons why women were able to enter and remain in the workforce included the availability of contraception. Before this time, women were expected to stay home and bear children to their husbands. The invention of the birth control provided women for the first time to have control over their bodies and livelihood. The contraceptive pill became FDA approved by 1963 and was also a key factor in providing women with independence and the ability to pursue professional careers without fear of losing their jobs because of pregnancy. The creation and availability of the birth control pill gave women sexual freedom and control over how they would live their lives without the help of a male which helped shift responsibility from one that had dependence solely on a man but one that became more of a partnership. Much controversy used to be associated to women who chose to postpone family obligations versus women who chose to pursue a career but over time the controversy has mostly disappeared. Women became role models to their daughters and the younger female population. This younger generation in the late 1950's and most of the 1960's would soon start women's liberation due to women recognizing the prejudices and discrimination that existed in the workplace when women began to seek advancement opportunities. Since then, Congress and the Equal Employment Opportunity Commission (EEOC) have passed many laws and regulations protecting women against sexual discrimination, unequal pay, and equality in the workplace. According to the U.S. Census (2000), Hispanic women still earned only 52 cents to every dollar by their white female counterpart and Hispanic men earned only 63 cents to every dollar earned by their white male counterpart. Hispanic workers were also more likely than their black or white counterparts to earn low incomes and be poor. This form of discrimination has been so subtle and often hard to prove but everyone was aware it was happening and not much has been done to change these irregularities in our workforce today.

Another area women fought hard to stop discrimination was in obtaining an education. For centuries, women were barred from attending universities or colleges until 1837 when Mary Lyon found Mount Holyoke in Massachusetts becoming the first four-year college exclusively for women. Women began to expand their education in areas such as business and science and began to see how crucial such knowledge brought to the workforce. Serving as role models in a limited capacity and also spreading this knowledge of independence to their own daughters drove home the importance having an education in order to attain better career choices. As the number of women increased in the workforce problems began to arise for many of them who attempted to move up the ladder or gain leadership positions because this was a new experience that many of the existing male leaders in the organization were not prepared to handle, or in some cases, did not want to address. This new type of organizational conflict against women attempting to attain upward mobility in business became known as hitting a glass ceiling.

Morrison and Von Glinow (1990) described this glass ceiling as a "concept popularized in the 1980's to describe a barrier so subtle that it is transparent, yet so strong that it prevents women and minorities from moving up in the management hierarchy" (p.200). Morrison et al (1987) further considered it as a barrier for women as a group, barring individuals' advancement simply because they are women rather than because they lack the ability to handle jobs at higher levels. This exclusion led to many disadvantages including limited knowledge of organizational happenings and forming alliances (Ibarra, 1993). It also prevented organizations from becoming radically different and for a period of time this was fine because globalization had not burst into the scene yet but the social demography was subtly changing.

Changes in the financial world would soon change this notion of complacency because around the world stock markets began to fall, large financial institutions collapsed or were bought out, and governments all over the world had to come up with ways to save their financial systems. Organizations quickly had to make adjustments in order to compete and stay financially afloat which led to changing the way business was done. Organizations and business were also facing serious consequences both legally and ethically when it came to justifying the lack of promotion opportunities for minorities and women in general. Chowdhury (2000) stated, "The most valuable commodity in business is not

technology or capital but people. The driving force behind a
21st century organization will be its people" p.10. In addition,
pressured by laws and interference by the federal government,
organizations and businesses had to make changes or begin to
face fines and penalties.

Companies also faced the possibility of having bad publicity
regarding discrimination reach the public and therefore losing
customer loyalty.

Businesses were also concerned with alienating the female
consumer. Senator Hillary Clinton's promise of universal
healthcare, changes to immigration system, and more affordable
education were key attractions to Hispanics in the last presidential
race. In addition to the fact that she would have been the first
female president in the White House made her even more popular
and the fact that many older generations tended to support her
because of the positiveness of better times when her husband
was president. The Clintons were a great example of the power
of the United States Hispanic vote. Furthermore, the location of
where Hispanics are residing also makes a difference. Hispanics
make up a big portion of the population in key voting states
such as New Mexico, Florida, Nevada, and Colorado which are
considered swing states in the political world.

Organizations and businesses realized they needed to conform
and make changes quickly. One way most organizations realized
they could make a difference was by looking at its internal talent and
leadership. Companies continue to be urged to support diversity
not solely because it was the law but because of economic and
ethical reasons (Cornelius & Gagnon, 2004; Weech-Maldonado
et al., 2002). Due to changing workforce demographics and
tougher business competition, organizations' interest had

increased in recognizing the value of a diverse workforce (Kirby & Harter, 2003). As the number of women, racial minorities, and immigrants had grown, companies responded by looking at their diversity management as a positive response in reaction to the controversies that surrounded affirmative action policies (Agocs & Burr, 1996). Organizations and businesses needed to know whether their workplace was advancing and promoting men and women in equal numbers in leadership, promotions, opportunities, and development (Rhode, 2003). The strategies and initiatives would need to be seen by the workforce, "as a catalyst, not as a substitute, for change, and they must be part of a systematic, sustained strategy" (p.27). Many businesses today have good intentions but their downfall sometimes lays in their inability to create a system of fair and equal practices that does help promote diversity in higher leadership positions. Some of these businesses and organizations also felt making an attempt was better than not making an attempt at all. Somehow it sometimes helped ease an organization's intents that they tried but other more pressing matters needed more attention and therefore tended to push diversity issues towards the bottom of the priority list.

While organizations are appearing to recognize that it makes good business sense to diversify their top management, underrepresentation of Hispanic women is a growing problem. This group of women represents a growing population in the workforce and as consumers. Organizations can no longer afford to ignore this group of people both in the workforce and as customers. One way organizations believe they can help improve diversity in higher leadership positions is through mentoring. Mentors can make a difference for those who are seeking to move up within the organization into future leadership positions. According to Wellington and Spence (2001), mentors make the difference for everyone. They are the people who can make a difference in advancement opportunities. Mentors most especially make a difference to this group of women who are relatively new to the professional business management workforce and have not had much guidance and support in their endeavors. The importance of matching up with a mentor who has a significant role in the organization with bright, educated Hispanic women could lead to interesting positive outcomes for the company because of the different perspective they are capable of providing based on their personal experience. The company is not aware of the advantages that can be possible if these opportunities are not explored much like Caucasian males have received in the past.

Most organizations and businesses came to see that whether fulfilling obligations or improving employee relations, mentoring had its advantages in helping to solve both of these major issues (Young, 2000; Lewis & Ferguson, 1995). The challenge for organizations is to understand the importance of mentoring and what it takes to provide mentoring that benefits both ends of the spectrum. Organizations also face difficulties in creating successful mentoring programs with positive outcomes and clear long term goals that will help improve the chances of high potential women in obtaining senior leadership positions.

Even more importantly, is the recognition that many of those women in the workforce today consists of the educated Hispanic female who is balancing home/work responsibilities. This is what sets today's workforce apart from yesterday's workforce. Yesterday's workforce had women who stayed home and ran the household while the male went to work and concentrated on his professional career. If this male happened to be young and Caucasian then his opportunities at advancement were even greater at moving up the corporate ladder. In comparison to today's workforce, most women are single and head of household and do not have a partner who is staying at home raising children and taking care of household responsibilities which is common among all ethnicities. While more men are more active in helping raise their children compared to the past, they most likely live in a separate household. For all intents and purpose of this book, I focus on the Hispanic female because they happen to be the fastest growing group in today's workforce and they also happen to be raising children at the same time. Today's companies need to be more cognizant of this fact by being more supportive and flexible with this type of workers. While it is happening across the board with all types of people, the fact that it is happening with this growing group of Hispanic women is significant to recognize that changes needed to happen. Organizations need to create mentoring programs that will help identify and support tomorrow's potential leader. Some industries such as healthcare are facing a crisis because along with costs, quality, infrastructure, and an aging population there is now a demand for significant change and strong leadership (Lantz, 2008). Organizations who are not tapping into their potential future talent pool may end up with catastrophic results. Most significantly, organizations should reflect the gender, racial, ethnic, and cultural diversity of the communities they serve (Dreachslin, 2007). Most often the representation only exists in entry level type positions. By having representation in mostly these two areas, Hispanic women have been prevented from accessing mentors, exposure to opportunity, and guidance. Despite the under representation in higher level executive positions, organizations get the whole idea of equal opportunity without regard to race, sex, religion, national origin, or disability but yet there is a real lack of Hispanics in senior executive positions in the United States. In the past, other barriers such as educational opportunities, racial discrimination, or working experience may have been reasons for under representation but do those reasons still apply?

The answer is no. As organizations become more complex the type of management competencies has drastically changed. It is for this reason companies need to work extra hard at attracting and retaining the brightest and most capable people which means human development (Zahra, 1999). At one time, organizations were based on norms and beliefs held and followed by men therefore creating masculine cultures which consisted of hidden assumptions, tacit norms and organizational practices that promoted forms of communication, views of self, approaches to conflict, images of leadership, organizational values, definitions of success and of good management which were stereotypically masculine (van Vianen & Fischer, 2002). Women who did not conform to these images were bypassed so only a small number of women reached executive levels (Mani, 1997). According to Mani, these organizations could no longer hold on to beliefs women lacked the ability to manage and motivate. Organizations or those in leadership positions also needed to overcome archaic beliefs that women are unable to overcome the challenge of balancing home and work.

These organizations are now facing a change in this makeup due to the increase of women in leadership roles with some companies. Beyond practicing affirmative action and equal opportunity requirements, organizations need to take a deep look at its internal pipeline and take some serious action. Yet, hesitation still occurs when looking at promotional opportunities for Hispanic women. Partly, this hesitation may be due to organizations and the people currently in positions of power who are afraid of change and how it may affect their role of power. Many business organizations have been run by the Caucasian male and there is no historical data significant enough to demonstrate success rate of organizations that have been run by women even more especially Hispanic women.

Organizations have had women in top CEO positions but not as prevalent as to the number of men who have held these positions. While slight progress has been made, women as CEO's continue to lag behind men when attaining these positions. Even more significantly are the number of Hispanic women who have attained CEO positions within organizations. Organizations continue to struggle with diversity in its leadership positions. Currently, only fifteen women serve as CEO's of Fortune 500 companies. That is only 3% of the largest US companies (retrieved on May 10, 2010 from *http://wexpo.biz/women_ceos*).

This is shocking data. How could this be happening in today's world? Unfortunately it is a sad realization that despite the progress, the Hispanic woman strongly feels we know we have personally made, we are still not recognized for the talent we are capable of offering and our innovative, creative way of handling matters. We ask only for an opportunity to demonstrate our capabilities and communicate our abilities. We understand our own personal barriers and have aggressively overcome them over the decades but to also have to face external barriers makes it more difficult. Interestingly, the one area where we have

---

---

made a significant change has been through the support of our President, Barack Obama. He elected the nation's first Hispanic Supreme Court Justice, Sonia Sotomayor. She is the third woman in court history. She is also known as saving America's favorite pastime, baseball. She was influential in ending baseball's strike back in 1995. A Hispanic woman who ended America's favorite pastime and becomes the nation's first Supreme Court Justice and organization's are still hesitant to place Hispanic women in leadership positions? Yes, this is one case but given an opportunity there could have been the possibility of so many more success stories. Yet, because of the majority's fear of change and sense of control stories such as these and opportunities that Sonia Sotomayor has experienced are rare in today's business world.

I think it also has to do with organizations stepping out of the norm and the loss of control by the elite group who are currently in positions of power. In the United States, Caucasian males are not a major representation of the current workforce or consumers. Organizations need to be very careful in investing in the right people and not excluding those who may also be able to contribute to a business' bottom line. Organizations need to be aware on how to attract, keep, manage, and identify talent that may potentially already exist in their workforce. In today's constantly dynamic business world, companies must recognize and be prepared to groom a different type of leadership. As long as Caucasian men continue to lead and own top senior level positions exclusively then equal opportunities will not be available for Hispanic women because organizations are not ready to accept that changes need to happen. The opportunity at senior leadership positions needs to be available to all who have the ability to lead regardless of their ethnicity, race, or gender. Even with the existence of discrimination laws, equal opportunity acts, more open and acceptance of minorities in the workforce, organizations are not ready to accept minority women into higher leadership roles.

How does an educated Hispanic woman in the workforce move up the ladder in this dynamic system? Are they encountering a glass ceiling? Are there any specific dynamic forces that are seen as external barriers to upward advancement? How important is having a mentor in the workplace to a Hispanic woman?

Chapter 2

Hispanic women in Today's Workforce: What does this mean?

Sadly compared to their female counterparts, Hispanic women face a tougher challenge in the workforce when it comes to pay and career advancements. Hispanic women earn considerably less than the Caucasian man and all other gender and cultural groups in the United States. According to the Institute for Women's Policy Research (September, 2010), Hispanic women earned only 52.9 cents for each dollar earned by white men. They are also viewed differently and face barriers including dissuasion and discrimination when it comes to obtaining an education, promotion, and balancing home/work obligations due to traditional culturally biased role assumptions. These are the constant internal and external barriers the Hispanic woman faces.

Hispanic women tend to be viewed as non-aggressive, under educated, and humble which are traits not normally tied in with leadership. Different studies have been conducted regarding leadership qualities and while women in general have been seen as not having traits tied to leadership, Hispanic women are even lower in the totem pole. While there has been much research made available on gender inequalities attributed to leadership (Prime, Carter, & Welbourne, 2009) there have also been a number of studies that have found the opposite to be quite true (Eagly et al., 2003; Eagly & Johnson, 1990). Some of these studies have revealed that qualities that in the past that have not been considered as leadership traits have in fact changed with the present workforce and are now considered to be traits necessary to leadership which men in general lack. Some of these leadership traits sometimes are divided between what Dev (2009) sees as women appearing to make decisions based on "feeling-oriented" and men's decision based on "thinking-oriented". Dev stated that it really is not so easily definable because most decision making is based on an individual's experience and skills that will guide them and not their preferred style. Concerning today's workforce this is very important because the workforce today is vastly different from what we consider to be yesterday's workforce. Today's workforce places as much importance to their personal responsibilities as they do to their professional/work responsibilities. Despite the steps today's workforce has done to educate themselves and gain necessary professional skills they still place just as much importance on their family responsibilities. Therefore, the belief that whether decisions are based on women's' "feeling oriented" or men's "thinking-oriented" begins to get blurred. It in fact becomes a blending of the two. While the workforce recognizes this to be true most companies are still struggling to understand and support. This lack of understanding is based on the fact of who is in charge and most likely it is a person who has not been in this type of situation.

Because this present workforce now includes a growing number of Hispanic women and have leadership traits that are considered as necessary, Hispanic women would appear to have an advantage. Because of their background, Hispanic women are accustomed to making decisions based on feeling, thinking, and experience which puts them in a unique position but has not been recognized just yet by most organizations. Some strides have been made that have opened opportunities for some women such as venturing to becoming entrepreneurs but for the most part challenges continue to present themselves to this group that makes it difficult to move forward in the corporate world where most of the counting is happening. Those opportunities often exist in entry level supervisor positions and not on higher level positions therefore often skewing data so that it appears that progress has been achieved when in fact it has not happened at all.

Changes in how women have been viewed and treated in the workforce have mostly happened due to factors such as changes in legal system (e.g., Civil Rights Act of 1964, affirmative action), equal opportunity practices, and changes in attitudes toward women. As more women have entered the workforce and the involvement of organizational initiatives such as diversity training have helped decrease negative views on women management capabilities, Hispanic women still lag behind any other group and continue to face barriers in upward professional mobility. They also at the same time face conflicts at home because traditional beliefs do not accept this modern behavior from Hispanic women.

Women, through time, have been considered as nurturers and lacking those leadership traits that in general portray an authoritive figure able to lead in decisive, concrete manner. Today's workforce benefits from a leader who is capable of demonstrating compassion, empathy, and also a sense of "Hey, I've been in those shoes" sense of understanding. Because this book is about Hispanic women in today's workforce, most of us as women have in some sense been in those shoes. Hispanic women since they were young have been instilled with this notion that raising a family is top priority. For some, because their parents came from another country where obtaining an education was not a priority, grew up in an environment where education came second to finding a job, raising a family, or being a family caregiver. Seeking an education was for some families seen as not necessary. These strong cultural expectations made it difficult for many Hispanic women to seek their own needs such as obtaining an education or pursuing a professional career.

Educational attainment for Hispanic women has been difficult to achieve. Because of their expected cultural role commitments other factors also come in to play. Most come from large families where there is no money for college. These families look favorably upon education but economic realities portray a different picture (Hite, 2007). Hispanic parents with high educational aspirations for themselves tended to have children with high levels of interest in college, whereas parents with minimal educational aspiration had children with similarly low or unidentified aspirations (Behnke, Piercy, & Diversi, 2004). For others, it was being raised by a single parent and facing responsibility so it meant going out to find a job. Most often it was hard labor for little pay but it meant supporting the family. Yet, for some Hispanic women who had mothers who had less than a high school education viewed what life may be like if they do not pursue a higher education thus increasing their motivation to pursue a higher education (Ojeda & Flores, 2008). As Hite (2007) noted, despite understanding how an education can better a Hispanic woman's future, economic and work environment become factors that hindered that pursuit.

Like most of their counterparts, Hispanic women in today's workforce realize that upward mobility means having a degree to support this movement in achieving a higher position. There has been an increase in Hispanic women seeking an education in the past decade but not at the same pace as the other gender and races. Therefore, this has made it difficult for Hispanic women to advance professionally in their careers. Many have and continue to face barriers when seeking higher level positions despite having the skills may not have the degree that may be required for the job.

When faced with these hurdles of difficulties in obtaining an education due to family obligations and lack of finances to obtain a degree, it does become difficult to pursue a higher level professional career or advance professionally for Hispanic women. The U.S. Census reported in 2009 that 13% of Hispanics over 18+ years old had at least a bachelor's degree or higher. The changes are slowly happening and there are reasons behind these changes that are causing the number of Hispanic women to increase in the workforce and slowly attain positions of higher ranking. Partly those reasons tend to be more Hispanics are earning a degree and entering the professional world with the aspiration of succeeding because attaining an education in America has been possible through educational financial aid programs which made it possible for U.S. citizens to seek college degrees.

Experiencing the responsibility of helping support their families from a young age and helping run a household has provided a Hispanic woman with a sense of capability, determination, and strength to face difficult challenges at a young age. This was often combined with expectations from family members who depended on these women to take care of things therefore giving Hispanic women an even bigger sense of responsibility and decision making power. Most had their mothers as role models who were raised in similar situations which tended to make some of them realize that this type of situation is not what they want for their future. They sought more both for personal and professional reasons.

Part of the uniqueness of a Hispanic woman is that they continue to maintain their family responsibilities but also now fulfill their desire for something more in their lives. These desires for many mean seeking higher education and obtaining a professional career. This has led to an incredible awareness of their capabilities in the workforce due to their past exposure in life. In addition, Hispanic women's experiences may be unique and different due to cultural and social group differences. They tend to have strong religious and community obligations in addition to their family responsibilities. Kamenou's (2008) study "indicated that in the world of work and the world of home were more distant in situations where ethnic minority women wanted to be active members in their ethnic groups" p.107. Because of these additional differences a greater barrier existed for Hispanic women who were attempting to balance home/work issues in the workforce.

While some may see the struggle of balancing work/personal life issues for Hispanic women it can actually be an advantage.

Without realizing it, they developed leadership skills which became an added benefit in the workforce. I have worked with many Hispanics in my career and it certainly has made my job easier. These women are self disciplined, committed, and loyal workers. What is striking about them is their ability to maintain a balance between home/work which proves their capabilities. Their ability to take control of the situation and assess needs requires leadership capabilities. Many organizations in today's business world recognize that it makes sense to acknowledge the fact that gender diversity is very important. Because women tend to have more responsibility to home/work issues many organizations need to create an atmosphere that tends to make it possible for them to be productive while fulfilling these responsibilities. These past two decades have shown that while the number of women has increased in the workforce it does not necessarily mean that organizations have made changes that reflect this unique group. In her work, Cabrera (2009) has found that workplace inflexibilities and lack of organizational support are driving women away creating a leaky pipeline of female talent and one, in which, organizations cannot afford to lose so much talent in today's competitive economy.

Cabrera's work discusses women who opt out of career paths when they find dissatisfaction with how the organization handles home/work balance issues but to Hispanic women this choice is not often the case because of economic and opportunity issues. Instead, they tend to hang in there and hope that an opportunity will surface down the road. The reason they tend to wait may be due to their sense of commitment and that both recognition and appreciation will be their reward in the end. Eng (2009) discussed the value of a fluent leader, "is to possess the skills and methods that allow one to understand and be understood across apparent borders" p.35. Fluent leaders understand the value of nuance, are outcome driven, deal with complexity, and are curious leaders who listen well. According to Eng, these fluency skills often come naturally to women and immigrants. I would say that it describes the leadership skills of a Hispanic woman.

In today's globalized economic environment that is constantly being faced with challenging changes, organizations are forced to increase their flexibility, innovativeness, and competitive edge. Some of these organizations are slowly discovering that the key lies in developing, supporting, and nurturing their employees who have increasingly become full of Hispanic women. It is no longer important to discover who is a better leader but more importantly, how do organizations support the growth of potential leaders who most likely could be a Hispanic woman? There was much debate as to which gender had better leadership capabilities in the past 20 years. Things have changed because organizations today are savvy enough to understand that individuals possess unique styles that can potentially provide a competitive edge regardless of their gender but why is there still hesitation when it comes to ethnicity, race, and gender?

Hollander and Yoder (1980) found role expectations, leadership style, and situational influences affect leadership that cause some women to become effective leaders while others may be less successful. Why is that so? Does it have anything to do with support and guidance some women may have received compared to others? In their study, Bergeron, Block, and Echtenkamp (2006) found the "think manager, think male" belief is still very true. Their research showed that women who were less female identified were less likely to experience stereotype threat than women who were more female identified. They described stereotype threat as a "threat of being at risk of conforming, as being true of oneself, a negative stereotype about one's group" p.134.

Could this be the case for Hispanic women when attempting to advance in the workplace? Do some Hispanic women face stereotype threat because of their difficulties in crashing the glass ceiling they encounter? Do they begin to doubt their own abilities to succeed? What else must they do to prove their capabilities?

The barrier that Hispanic women face is the opportunity to get to this point where they are able to demonstrate their abilities if given the chance and most importantly the opportunity. Certainly when faced with constant barriers and disillusions regarding their quest at advancement it would seem natural that one would begin to doubt one's own capabilities. When you add the additional responsibilities that Hispanic face (responsibilities and expectations at home, religious beliefs, and traditional values) it can be overwhelming. For some, they settle and accept the situation. This does not mean they give up but for some it may not be the time to fight so they bide their time and concentrate on other areas of their life such as raising a family or expanding their education. Some of these Hispanics see it as an opportunity to get stronger and better so fewer excuses can be given to them as to why they cannot advance in their careers when the time comes. Like many other women, Hispanic women tend to also have feelings of burnout. Work related psychological disorders are a leading disease in the U.S. according to the National Institute for Occupational Safety and Health (Sauter, Murphy, & Hurrell, 1990). Burnout can cause fatigue, depression, and emotional exhaustion, and reduced perceptions of personal accomplishment. Because Hispanic women represent a small token of the workforce they tend to be under more scrutiny and pressure than their peers. Over time, the pressure becomes overwhelming and leads to burnout. At some point, decisions need to be made if risking your health is worth the trouble of seeking equal opportunity in the workplace.

In their research, Hernandez and Morales (1999) interviewed Hispanics who described in their path to further their careers that there exists these ladders with rungs that have barriers that need to be climbed where eventually they are boxed into positions the organization stereotypically feels Hispanics should be doing rather than the work the individual actually feels they are capable of doing therefore encountering this glass ceiling that is not easily provable as discriminatory. It is a very common practice that has not been able to be proven yet it happens and wonder if this has anything with the barriers to advancement opportunities for Hispanic women.

Like most Hispanics in other organizations, the study participants in Hernandez and Morales research cited the lack of role models. When some Hispanic women choose to exit this environment they are perceived by the organization as an inability to succeed but which is often not the case. Having a mentor is associated with career and organizational advancement. It is a fact that women have more difficulty of finding a mentor in the workplace compared to men due to various reasons. Some of these reasons include lack of female role models or the difficulty in still accepting women as role models. However, mentors maybe should be white males because they are still the majority in representing leadership positions in the workforce.

They still continue to be the ones who hold positions of power and influence. They are also the most recognized and have valuable information concerning the organization. If aligned with this type of mentor, Hispanic women can gain greater access to information, exposure, and opportunity. The difficult part comes in pairing a Hispanic woman with a Caucasian male mentor who understands and can empathize with a Hispanic woman's cultural background. These women did not grow up in the same type of environment and may never fit in with the good old boys' network. In these cases, it may be best to find two types of mentors that would satisfy both professional and personal needs.

In some cases where mentoring is available, the type of mentoring is often inadequate. By this I mean the type of mentoring senior mentors believe they should provide include help with public speaking, working on their resumes, helping them create Excel or Word spreadsheets, how to help create proposals, social networking, or how to manage their time. This is the wrong type of mentoring to provide to Hispanic women who have considerable work and educational experience. Most have already been exposed and have experience in these areas already. Senior mentors are out of the loop as to what most people have learned in school and also what they have experienced in their prior jobs. This may be due to the lack of preparedness by mentors or by the organization when it comes to mentoring. For some, it appears to be an afterthought or another job duty.

Because of the lack of support, mentors often appear to follow a connect the dot type of approach to mentoring. An approach they feel that their mentee can easily follow and also give the sense of satisfaction that mentor has satisfied their responsibility.

This type of mentoring lacks direction, motivation, inspiration, and satisfaction. Mentees walk away feeling disappointed and often feeling undermined because they were not taken seriously. Having been one of those Hispanic women who has had a mentor I can recall my own experiences. While I like to walk away from every experience as to having learned something, I often walked away feeling more despondent and dejected. I then realized that in most of my formal mentoring experiences there was a lack of a game plan. I never felt that my experience was going to end up with my career taking off in the right direction but more because the organization felt they were doing the right thing of attempting to support me. The problem with this was that what was most important to me as a Hispanic woman in the workplace was to move my career in an upwards direction not stabilize me to where I presently stood. I felt this was the most frustrating part and generally what research proves regarding boxing Hispanics into certain positions they feel we belong.

Even more frustrating is this sense of being stuck. Eventually, most of us do decide to leave and instead concentrate on growing our careers in another manner. Fighting both gender and racial economic disparities has made Hispanics seek alternative solutions. Some organizations are realizing they are losing talented individuals due to a lack of formal mentoring programs in the workforce. It is a step in the right direction and one that will provide Hispanic women with hope that they will eventually see positive results. So, what does this mean to Hispanic women in today's workforce seeking upward mobility?

It means that more than ever there is a way to make an impact because we have all the necessary tools, resources, and legal rights to break barriers or shatter this so called glass ceiling. It has not been easy and it will continue to be a struggle. I think the major difference is that because many of us have spent so much time and money furthering our education while continuing to work, we cannot afford to quit at this point. We cannot give up what we have put so much effort on when it comes to pursuing a career. The struggle for us has been balancing an education, work, and family and therefore we are better prepared to handle barriers that exist in promotion opportunities. Slowly but surely as data has revealed, the number of Hispanic women are attaining higher education and obtaining professional jobs. We need to continue to question why we are being overlooked for promotion opportunities. We also need to push for mentoring support. We need to push businesses and organizations to take responsibility and provide equal opportunity towards minority women such as Hispanic women towards executive leadership positions. Lastly, we need to know we have support from those organizations we have put considerable effort and dedication and feel that there is a light at the end of the tunnel.

In the next chapter, I will be discussing organizational responsibility. How do organizations handle or recognize internal growth? What is an organization's responsibility to its workforce regarding development? Are organizations invested in creating mentoring programs to help support and guide minority women such as Hispanic females who have the background (education, experience, skills) to get ahead?

Chapter 3

Organizational Responsibility

Over the years, I have read many books and articles relating to management style and effective leadership and I have to say many have made an impression. I have also put many to use with success. Most distinctively, I have found those researchers and writers who distinguish between management and leadership has made the most impression. I do not recall who exactly said that there is a big difference between being a manager and being a leader but I certainly recall that when I read that statement I made a decision about being a leader versus being a manager. I knew I wanted to be someone who wanted to make a difference not just someone who could follow orders. I feel that there is a clear distinguishment between the two (management and leadership) and therefore will discuss both in this section because organizations and businesses need to recognize who in their workforce best fits each of these roles. Hispanic women need to also recognize the difference between the two so they can make decisions based on where they are on the totem pole and where they are personally. I say this because at some point you need to have done both styles, learned the styles each one requires, recognize the difference, and make a decision as to what best suits you at a certain point in your life. I was fortunate enough to have experienced both in my personal and professional life. In each scenario, I gained a wealth of knowledge that I strongly feel I have used to my advantage and what has best suited my needs and for the organization I worked. It was certainly a learning process but well worth it in the end. I will begin by discussing management styles.

There have been several management styles each with own uniqueness that suited the times. Beginning with Scientific Management back in the early 1900's and led by Frederick Winslow Taylor, Taylorism Management Style believed in management making all the decisions and developing a standard method to perform each job. Taylorism also favored selecting employees with certain abilities who were capable of being trained using standard measures. Taylorism method was also one of the first to introduce incentives into the workforce. This style placed importance on training and providing necessary tools for employees to do their job.

This was followed by a similar style of management called Fayolism which was introduced by Henry Fayol in the 1920's. Fayolism had certain principles of administration such as division of labor, top management authority, employee discipline, and the belief the organization had a responsibility towards employees such as the provision of resources, job descriptions, encouragement of thinking outside box, and quality control. Fayolism also argued that a manager also had responsibilities they needed to maintain. This type of management was not based solely on the employees shoulder but managers also had to carry their weight. Managers were expected to be healthy, clever, have morals, cultural knowledge, management capacity, competent, and have the strongest skills. This style of management placed importance on managers and not just the workers.

A third early 20th Century style of management was the Hawthorne Effect developed in the 1930's and 1940's led by Elton Mayo. This style of management led by experimentation believed in keeping employees happy. Mayo conducted experiments where the introduction of breaks, providing food, interviewing employees, and payment incentives were tested to see end results. The Hawthorne Experiments proved to the corporate world that people were the main resources for any organization when treated with attention and appreciation and if they were kept happy then productivity would remain high. This was probably the first example of motivation in the workforce.

This was followed by Maslow's Theory on the Hierarchy of Needs. Maslow's Theory to this day is widely known throughout the world. Maslow's Theory was based on a set of principles that people absolutely rate according to importance. At the top, people need to have their physiological needs met such as food, shelter, clothing, and warmth. According to Maslow's Theory, a person's motivation begins with satisfying these needs. Once physiological needs are satisfied, people then need to take care of their safety needs such as personal, financial, and health. This is then followed by social needs such as friends, intimacy, relationships, and family. The next step in Maslow's Hierarchy concerned people needing to feel accepted and respected. Lastly, there remained a people actualization need which was the need to identify and realize their maximum potential. People who reached this stage had a high level of self motivation.

In the 1950's we heard the word empowerment introduced by Peter Drucker. Drucker believed empowered employees ended up contributing to the organization's success (Drucker, 2008). Drucker strongly believed motivation of employees, excellent communication, coordination and clarity of goals were three important governing principles in an organization's success. Today, the business world has grown into an extremely challenging field with many unique management styles. Most of these I feel are insufficient or inadequate because they do not reflect today's workforce. Drucker once wrote "Indeed, reality is fast becoming the very opposite of what these assumptions claim to be" p. 5. I tend to agree because today's employees tend to need to know how to manage themselves.

I believe this is the case due to longer life spans where people have been exposed to more knowledge, skills, independence, and realities that may not have been as prevalent in the past. Another reason could be that most people do not spend their entire career with one company so they end up gaining different skills as they continue to move.

After Drucker's empowerment theory, a few other styles came into existence which included authoritarian, democratic, paternalistic styles, and many more. Somehow whether paternalistic, authoritarian, none appear to satisfy the management style and how it relates to the Hispanic women who is present in today's workforce and her journey towards upward mobility. Is this partly due to the fact that organizations continue to fail to recognize and acknowledge a different workforce has emerged? I wonder if the recognition is on purpose or it really is ignorance. It is hard to believe leaders in higher level positions could ignore what is evident as to how important is the Hispanic woman in today's workforce. Hispanic women have major influence as both consumers and as part of the workforce. For Hispanic women to continue to face barriers to upward mobility or for an organization to fail to recognize the importance of having Hispanic women in leadership positions could possibly lead to missed opportunities with recognizing future talent that can contribute to the organization's success. It is a lost opportunity at having a business advantage plus it is ethically wrong because equal opportunities are not being allotted to all. Sooner or later, organizations need to realize that they are not fulfilling their commitment at improving diversity in senior leadership positions.

It is a sad reality that Hispanic women who have the education, skills, and experience must still struggle to attain higher leadership positions in today's business world compared to other races and ethnic backgrounds. I have mentioned the importance of mentoring programs to help Hispanic women but cannot help but recognize that compared to Caucasian males, why do Hispanic women need to go through so much just to be recognized for their abilities? Why is it still a problem to have diversity in higher leadership positions?

When will equal opportunity really begin to exist? In the American workforce today there is representation of the population and organizations that do not take advantage of their diverse workforce and help them advance into senior leadership positions are missing opportunities. Companies need to groom and develop Hispanic women into leadership positions not just because they are doing it for their own personal reasons but because their customers are looking for it (Pyrillis, 2011). Because customers are looking for diversity and Hispanic females are the fastest growing group in the workforce and newly powerful consumers means that businesses need to have improved and effective plans in retention, training and development for this particular group and not continue to provide opportunity exclusively to Caucasian males.

Leadership in the workforce

Zaleznik (1977) wrote that leaders seek opportunities. They are change agents versus managers who seek to follow the rules. Leaders tend to be innovators while managers tend to adhere to guidelines. At some point in our professional careers and our drive to succeed, we have worn both hats. In the end, most of us want to be considered as leaders.

Magretta (2002) asked "What does respect for the individual mean and how is it translated into management practice?" p.206. Magretta stated that it boils down to accepting that each person is different and therefore good at different things and that what matters most to performance is getting the right individual for the job. Therefore, it is management's role to spot talent and put it where it can contribute to performance. This is also supported by Charan, Drotter, and Noel (2001) who stated, "The more people achieve, the more learning takes place; willingness to tackle new challenges increases as current challenges are met" p.6. Charan, Drotter, and Noel believed that to capitalize on these potentials then organizations should be capable of recognizing what is needed to make the transition from one level to the next. The key is to recognizing the type of people that are in the workforce today such as the Hispanic woman and providing opportunities for them. It is important for organizations to understand that workforce demographics have changed and that equal opportunity must be given to this new emerging workforce. It could be a workforce that presents new ideas or ways of doing things that they could in return learn and gain new perspectives.

Individuals who aim to succeed have for the most part an idea of what they need to do in both their personal and professional lives to fulfill their quest. These are those so called internal and external barriers. When making plans that will impact their professional career, an individual will want then to work for an organization they feel could be the place where they can use their potential to make a difference. Unfortunately what happens with Hispanic women is that at some point they encounter a brick wall. It should be at this point that organizations have a responsibility to invest in their employees and prevent these invisible barriers from preventing professional growth of the individual. Thomas and Gabarro (1999) identified some of these invisible and visible barriers into three categories of which the first was the prevalence of prejudice followed by issues of comfort and risk, and lastly the difficulty of identifying high-potential minorities. Thomas and Gabarro wrote that the prejudices that exist in the workforce are not necessarily coming from individuals but rather from a more dominant powerful group within the organization that has certain assumptions pertaining to a particular group in the workforce. The second, subtle barrier that existed involved comfort and risk amongst senior members working with members who were of a different racial group which often resulted in discomfort, feelings of alienation, and pressure on both ends. Lastly, Thomas and Gabarro acknowledged that based on the systematic prejudices added with comfort and risk led to difficulties in assessing minority potential. This then led to the fact that it became a difficult path for minorities to move into senior leadership positions. These three invisible and visible barriers are very common and true. The funny thing about them is that they are often so subtle that in many cases they can cause an individual to wonder if they are imagining if it is actually happening. This may lead to resentment, underperformance, and feelings of insecurity for the individual. These individuals end up staying in these positions until they regain their sense of confidence and motivation to again venture forth in their quest to move up the ladder once again. Sometimes this time of regrouping and planning provides the individual with a better outlook on what their goals are for their future. Most often it results in leaving their place of employment and seeking an opportunity elsewhere.

Otherwise, these employees will demonstrate their commitment, loyalty, knowledge, and leadership to get ahead and help the organization succeed but they need the organization to help support their development. One such way that an organization can demonstrate its commitment to improving diversity in senior leadership is through its leadership pipeline. Charan, Drotter, and Noel call it the Leadership Pipeline. They stated the Leadership Pipeline is about organizations identifying leadership candidates early, providing them with growth assignments, giving them useful feedback, and coaching them. This all leads to mentoring identifying potential people who are going to make a difference to the organization. For those Hispanic women who have been intertwining their personal and professional capabilities this is critical. It means organizations and businesses will begin to recognize the contribution a Hispanic woman is capable of providing. People development in an organization or business demonstrates how important its employees are to the company and that the company recognizes potential talent. It also acknowledges that the organization is open to change.

The development of an internal pipeline leads to higher morale, increased productivity and commitment, improved communications, and lower staff turnaround. Mentors are people who can help people grow professionally and personally. An organization or business that provides mentoring to its employees who are interested in moving up the leadership path is taking action and strategically planning ahead. Mentors can help individuals become better leaders by showing them how to navigate the formal and informal cultures of the organization. This is especially important to Hispanic women who have not always been provided with this type of guidance in a formal setting such as in the work environment. Businesses also recognize the importance of mentoring to this particular group of people because improving diversity into higher leadership roles ultimately leads to adaptability to an ever changing environment. Recognizing the fact that it is an ever changing environment leads to identifying demographic buying trends, product marketability, and customer needs. Mentors often are able to identify individuals who can get the job done.

Organizations who are committed to improving diversity in higher level of management as a valuable asset understand the importance of staying competitive. When top management supports and encourages diversity it becomes clear to the rest of the organization that change is happening in the way things have traditionally been happening. It is a gradual shift taking place within the organization and part of the reason women have begun to move up the corporate ladder over time. It has also been the reason organizations have begun to acknowledge the importance of having women mentors team up with potential future female leaders. This acceptance of encouraging differences leads to new ideas and can provide competitive advantages for the organization.

The alignment of female mentors with potential future female leaders that have been identified within the organization is an important action an organization can do to increase diversity such as having more Hispanic women have an opportunity at higher level positions. Is this sufficient action to increase opportunities for Hispanic women to professionally grow within the organization? What actions does an organization or business need to really do to show its commitment to increasing Hispanic women opportunities in business? How much does a Hispanic woman need to do to be recognized in order to get ahead in an organization? In the end, do Hispanic women have to conform to certain roles and rules in order to be accepted? How much change must happen in an organization in order to recognize the importance of diversity in leadership positions? These questions and more will be addressed in the next section of this chapter.

Importance of mentoring in an organization

Having done previous research on mentoring, I am a big proponent of it. I especially believe it is beneficial to Hispanic women seeking upwards mobility in an organization and working in an environment where they are able to balance both their personal and professional lives. As previously mentioned, there are the obvious benefits of mentoring such as networking, learning the ropes, understanding the culture, and one-on-one teachings but mentoring especially to Hispanic women is critically important in how it is delivered and what will be the outcome. The importance is in the recognition by the organization that new players have entered the game that require a different level of support, training, and understanding because it is a new generation in a vastly different business world compared to ten to fifteen years ago. Businesses have the added challenge of not only facing a dynamic new workforce but also balancing this workforce with a volatile business environment. In the past, the business world was able to enjoy and maintain a certain type of workforce and concentrate on other aspects of business such as the technology boom and global impact. Yet, steadily and quietly, a new workforce was slowly but surely developing that I strongly believe the business world never expected and that is the emergence and impact of the Hispanic woman in the business world. This workforce includes Hispanic women who place as much importance on their personal responsibilities as they do on their professional ones.

Businesses today have their hands full with meeting these challenges. Mentoring is one major way an organization can begin to face these challenges. By pairing up mentors with potential talent, organizations can help speed up the process of preparing leaders who will be able to deal with these challenges happening in the business world. Mentors should be individuals who are capable of teaching and guiding future leaders in such a way as to inspire success and a desire to develop and grow within the company. The alignment of a mentor with a Hispanic woman provides a clearer sense of direction for this group of women who have never really been on this route before. They end up with a sense of justification and satisfaction that the organization has invested time and money in their development and that the organization cares about this particular group's success. Once again it brings attention to the fact that organizations and businesses are recognizing the importance of Hispanic women in today's business and workforce.

I have had the experience of working with mentors in the workplace and have absolutely walked away with a positive experience. Besides the benefits of networking, honing my professional social skills, and becoming a part of the culture, I felt I learned to be accepted and acknowledged which I strongly do not feel I would have been as successful if I had ventured out alone. This is not to say that every mentor I had was fabulous but even the not so great ones provided a learning opportunity. Collins and Porras (1994) wrote "Visionary companies develop, promote, and carefully select managerial talent grown from inside the company to a greater degree than the comparison companies" p. 173. Collins and Porras revealed the importance of preserving the core of a company which can only be done when a company invests on internal talent. Providing mentoring helps maintain continuity because the mentee is thrust into the culture of the company, the day-to-day functionalities, introduction to key people who make things happen, and at the same provide exposure for the mentee. This is critical information for organizations who want to help develop leaders and not just managers. While change is important and not to be ignored, creating a succession plan is necessary in order to maintain core values because the organization has invested on individuals who have been with the company long enough to comprehend its culture and values. When you combine a successful succession plan involving mentoring with a changing workforce that has individuals who have not been given an opportunity at leadership may lead to opportunities at being ahead of the competition. The key is in providing an opportunity to showcase the capabilities of educated, skilled, experienced Hispanic women who work in these organizations with a chance to learn at a higher level the ins and outs of the company so that eventually they are able to contribute to the success of the company and clearly support their leadership abilities. When Hispanic women are exposed to this different level of experience progress is happening.

Having a positive mentoring experience is very important but may not always happen. Often, the mentee is eager, highly intelligent, motivated, energized in learning whatever may come their way. Eventually, the mentee may surpass the mentor and lead to feelings of betrayal, anger, and rejection on the mentor's part. This reaction is not done on purpose from either party but may result from natural outcomes. It is important for both parties to recognize what the final outcome may be from the beginning and to discuss final results. Organizations often fail to implement a plan from the onset detailing a plan of action with clear outcomes. Mentors are not prepared in advance to understand and realize why mentees are being prepped. Mentors and mentees may also have different agendas as to why they are involving themselves in a mentoring partnership. In this respect, it is an organization's responsibility to provide a clear, comprehensive mentoring program where both parties understand and realize what their partnership is going to accomplish. My research has shown that mentoring programs often fail because there is no clear distinguishment on goals and outcomes for either party. Often both mentees and mentors walk away from their experience feeling they wasted their time or worse, they did not learn any valuable lessons.

I mentioned feelings of resentment on mentor's part which may be result of misunderstandings or unclear objectives that I need to clarify. Most mentors certainly do not feel this way but may be a result, as mentioned, of objectives and outcomes not clearly defined before mentoring relationship has begun between both parties. Mentors are usually individuals who have been with the organization for a long time and are asked to share their knowledge and help groom new talent. Some mentors depending where they are in their professional stage are happy to oblige because they are near retirement and have the organization's best interest at heart and want to help out. Yet, because of longer life spans which have caused individuals to work into their much later years, mentors may feel that their organization is sublimely trying to push them out. It is critical for an organization to clearly explain that this is not the case and that they value the mentor as much as they value the development of future leaders. Organizations need to be proactive in explaining and demonstrating the importance of both mentors and mentees to an organization's future success.

Once a mentor is assured that the intent is not to replace them, mentors are able to share knowledge willingly without the fear they are being replaced. Mentors should be individual's who have been given clear guidance and support to provide the best type of teaching, support, and guidance to their mentees because the outcome benefits everyone involved in the process. Often organizations believe mentors should just "go ahead . . . . show the new kid the ropes" but this is not the way to approach mentoring relationships. Mentoring partnerships is so much more. Charan, Drotter, and Noel (2001) agreed development must continue until full performance has been reached because incremental improvement is insufficient "This acceptance is easier when organizations see full performance as a competitive advantage rather than some technical human resources concept" p.154. I think today's workers are savvier about knowing the difference of when an organization is truly committed to their development and perhaps contributes to final outcome of where their commitment will be directed towards. In their book, "In Search of Excellence", Peters and Waterman (2004) discuss how in the 1980's Japan became front runners in management practices due to their approach to workforce and quality because they recognized the most natural resource is its people "loyalty, commitment through effective training, personal identification with the company's success and, most simply, the human relationship between the employee and his supervisor" p. 39. These are important items to consider as a new wave of workers and potential leaders are in today's workforce such as the Hispanic woman. Based on management books on how to identify effective and potential leaders that have been written in the last 30 to 40 years, we are once again facing a new trend. Organizations have been recognizing this shift in the workforce for the past 15 years but have failed in creating effective internal pipeline development processes. For women such as myself, it has been frustrating remaining in organizations where there appears to be no professional upward mobility prospects. Because this type of barrier is often so sublime and hard to prove, Hispanic women tend to give up. By simply providing mentoring and through a good mentoring program, organizations can adequately provide an opportunity for Hispanic women to grow within the company. In return, it also provides the organization with an opportunity to also learn from this unique group.

Mentoring programs in the business world today

Organizations simply need to create, develop, and sustain mentoring programs that have an impact. Mentors must be provided with a complete training on mentoring. Mentors will need to be provided with complete comprehensive management diversity trainings. Mentors must also be provided with justifications and compensations for the added responsibility they will be taking on in their new role. Mentors selected should also be assessed to see if they have the necessary qualifications and capabilities of becoming a mentor. Mentoring requires teaching, supporting, and guiding other individuals and not every senior, experienced person who has been with the organization may have these skills. In some cases, individuals who have been identified as potential mentors may not choose to be involved and this is why candidates selected should be based on participation with compensation. Compensation is absolutely necessary because mentors will be taken on additional responsibility and to guarantee that there are participants available.

Mentoring programs in the business world with today's diversified workforce is absolutely critical and it has to be done correctly. It can no longer be an informal process where a new employee follows an experienced, older individual as he walks around pointing the ins and outs of the company. Organizations need to be able to provide formal mentoring with clear goals and solid identifiable outcomes because if they are not successful they face retention issues and credibility. Mentoring programs should also have an outcome where if done correctly and progress and development is evident results in a shift in diversity representation in higher level executive positions. I have seen mentoring programs in organizations where mentees are not given any guarantee or prospect at attaining a promotion or upward mobility opportunities. I have been involved and seen how mentees were given praised, patted on the back, given thumbs up recognition but continued to remain in the same entry-level position. This makes absolutely no sense at all. Why would any aspiring individual hoping to grow with the organization and recognized by the organization as a mentee go through the motions of being mentored when there is no guarantee that there is a possibility that they will be promoted or rise into senior rank positions? Having interviewed mentees in my prior research, the reaction has been disbelief, anger, sense of betrayal, waste of time, and discouragement. Incredibly, many companies continue to believe their policies around promotion does not need to change in order to improve diversity in higher level management positions to reflect historically underrepresented groups (*www.hewittassociates.com*).

A cultural change at a higher level needs to happen. Companies spend millions of dollars on diversity programs, appointing diversity officers, send their executives to diversity conferences and seminars, and keep diversity scorecards and yet companies continue to lack real and effective practices concerning the promotion of diversity in senior level positions. The concern is that there is no hard evidence that all these practices are making a difference but yet discrimination suits filed with the Equal Employment Opportunity Commission are on the rise. Companies have been attempting to handle diversity issues for some time now but evidence shows not much difference has happened despite all the efforts. What is going to make the difference with today's organizations tackling diversity issues differently with real positive results? It is difficult to measure this type of cultural and diversity change in a quantitative manner so that organizations are able to actually measure if training and education has been successful or unsuccessful. Who ultimately makes decision on how much effort is going to be placed on improving diversity representation in higher level positions and how will this process be measured for success? I strongly believe that changes happen when an organization's top senior leaders make it a priority. The business world today is incredibly tumultuous and improving diversity in senior level position could take a back seat if the company chose to do so but does not go down this path. A company that is strongly committed in making changes will not be deterred from its course of action. This represents true commitment by the company that it is serious about something they feel has to change.

The change will not happen overnight for Hispanic women attaining higher level executive positions. Some may feel the wait has been too long already and I would agree but we have to acknowledge the advancements we have already made however hard and difficult the journey has been compared to other races and ethnicities. There is now hard data reflecting the underrepresentation of Hispanic women in executive positions despite their growth in the workforce. Combined with their added skills, knowledge, and education these forces are bringing much needed attention to the lack of diversity in higher level senior positions in businesses. In addition, the personal strength Hispanic women possess makes them more vocal about their dissatisfaction with attaining these higher level executive positions that many can no longer ignore. Combined with

Hispanic women's formidable spending consumer power which stands at over $1.0 trillion dollars of which Hispanic women account for approximately one-third of this total at $330 billion (Selig Center, Package facts, 2009). Hispanic women can no longer be a group organizations can ignore regarding promotion and mentoring opportunities. Now the difference will be in how organizations respond to this new emerging workforce and how serious and committed they are about acknowledging and accepting the change. Hispanic women today have done more than their peers to get ahead in the business world. They have been able to maintain their personal family obligations, earn higher education degrees, and concentrated on their professional careers simultaneously without losing a sense of who they are and what they want to accomplish. This is tremendous work that involves a higher degree of motivation, determination, and strength that many people are not capable of handling. Hispanic women also clearly understand that for many of us, we know what is important in our lives (such as our families) and Hispanic women realize that we must make difficult decisions but what has changed over time has been that we value our family obligations more than we do our professional careers.

Organizations recognize they need to diversify their higher leadership roles with HR strongly encouraging this need but to no avail in most cases. Ultimately, the decision maker who is most often a Caucasian male selects someone who has had prior experience in an executive role. The problem is despite more Hispanic women interviewing for these positions most of us do not have a lengthy record of executive experience because we have not been given the opportunity at upward mobility. Therefore, Hispanic women may be interviewing and aiming for higher positions but in the end they continue to be passed over for someone else who has had some prior experience. It appears organizations are not yet ready to take a chance on having Hispanic women in senior leadership positions. Organizations need to make a major overhaul in order to begin to recognize the importance of diversity in higher leadership positions.

It is a different world today. Women have come a long way in the business world. Yet, for the Hispanic woman there has not been much formal progress or opportunities but on a smaller more personal way there has been change. We appear to fulfill the entry level role but any higher the door is still firmly shut. Unlike any other class, race, or gender, Hispanic women have shown their value in both their personal and professional lives. Hispanic women have broken through the barrier but still face hardship trying to seek higher level positions in organizations. While there have been a number of Hispanic women who made significant strides in their fields, Hispanic women still drastically lag behind any other group when it comes to executive positions. Hispanic women are determined to get professionally ahead and be recognized for their commitment and contributions. They may seek an alternate route such as starting their own business or seeking employment with a new organization but they will not give up the notion of seeking higher level positions. Simply put, they have placed too much time, effort, and sacrifice to just step aside. This next section will discuss the impact of facing barriers to higher level positions has had on Hispanic women in the business world.

Chapter 4

Impact on Hispanic Women

Probably the hardest impact a Hispanic woman faces in her professional career is the disappointment that they have not broken through promotion barriers in the workforce. Hispanic women have faced and handled difficult challenges in their personal lives and taken measurements such as expanding their education to ensure that when they seek higher level positions they will have a better chance at success. Reaching for this idea of success ends up most often as a hopeless cause because the constant barriers Hispanic women have to face eventually leads to disappointment, burnout, and frustration. Hispanic women who face these challenges can only keep up with this pace of attempting to be recognized yet the effects of balancing home/work issues for a certain amount of time becomes too much before something has to give and takes priority. Most often it leads to Hispanic women moving on and seeking opportunities elsewhere or in certain growing cases in recent years, becoming entrepreneurs.

Women tend to seek more value into their personal and holistic needs rather than to the growth of an enterprise especially when that organization is not invested in its workforce. Hispanic women therefore choose to leave their jobs and move towards a goal where they feel they will have more control over their happiness and face new challenges. Hispanic women will also tend to feel a better balance between their home and work as a result of the action they took to take control of their professional lives. Hispanic women who chose to seek entrepreneurship also felt they had better control on their earnings. In 2007, there were 7.4% Hispanic women who considered themselves self-employed (US Department of Commerce). Despite the difficulties in starting your own business, many Hispanic women strongly felt that being in complete control was well worth the difficulties of starting their own business. It can be challenging raising the capital, acquiring bank loans, long hours, and facing the uncertainty of failure but mostly the thrill of realizing that by being their own boss there has been a difference in their professional live. In order for organizations stop this significant workforce from leaving they must do certain things.

It is important for organizations to communicate to its staff how important they are to the company. This is a fact. It boils down to companies demonstrating how important and valuable their employee is to the organization. When this is not shown or communicated to an individual then the individual loses trust and commitment. Valuing an employee means demonstrating commitment to an employees' success, offering guidance and developmental support, and creating an environment that supports that individual's growth. Valuing and understanding that supporting employees is important is still something that companies still fail to accomplish. Value is extremely important and when this is not communicated successfully to employees then lack of commitment, trust, and belief may be felt by the employee. These employees will seek to find an organization that is willing to invest and listen to them.

The effects of losing talented employees on organizations ends up costing the company billions of dollars on recruiting new hires due to worker retention issues. Appreciating and respecting generates the same type of feeling in return which affects the organization's performance and productivity. Companies often react too little and too late. More sadly, businesses continue to make the same mistake over and over again. Due to this lack of appreciation and value and facing pressure with home responsibilities, Hispanic women tend to move on and make changes in their lives that will be less stressful and more rewarding. Having had many conversations with these women I have found that they have taken too many steps in their lives to be successful women to have to then face this type of disappointment in the workplace. These women do not have to accept these conditions based on what they are capable of doing, what they have achieved, and where they aim to be with their professional goals.

Another type of impact on Hispanic women being overlooked in the workforce results in women receiving the necessary experience to move towards leadership positions. Minority women will then need to look and take their skills and apply it towards a company they hope and believe will provide them with the opportunity at working in an environment that will help them gain the necessary experience to grow. Sometimes it will take more than a few places to find a place that will eventually provide this experience for minority women because some of these companies recognize the value in investing in this dynamic new workforce.

Unfortunately for some of these companies who are not taking appropriate action at improving leadership diversity is that they end up losing credibility. Because most likely these organizations end up failing to initiate and implement successful diversity programs, word spreads quickly about the organization's lack of commitment at supporting minorities in higher level positions. Organizations face the risk of losing the opportunity at hiring potential talent because of its lack of credibility regarding supporting diversity in its workforce. Because of the wealth of knowledge and accessibility of information most people are aware of organizations' reputation and where they stand with supporting its workforce. Regardless of the economic, social, political, and technological changes in the workforce at this time, people today still strongly believe they have the ability to make an educated choice about whom and where they will work nowadays which includes Hispanic women. There are also many networking and social networks out there that help keep people informed as to which companies are invested in promoting diversity in higher leadership roles.

Hispanic women realize that attempting to meet an organization's expectation such as getting involved in more challenging work, developing a style that white male or female managers are comfortable with, working extra hard or going that extra mile, expanding your network does not really make a difference. Because historically Hispanic women have not been in the professional workforce too long their networking circle is not as expansive as those of white men in the business world. I remember once interviewing for a position for a senior director position and the man who interviewed was asking me about my background. I happen to ask him how he ended up in his position and he mentioned he had known the chief financial officer. I remember thinking how wonderful it must be to have such connections. Coincidentally, the CFO was also a white male. It was at this moment that I realized that what I had read about minorities attempting to attain higher leadership positions is difficult due to who is making decisions. White males are making decisions and they feel comfortable hiring other while males or those that think and act similar to them.

This led me to believe what a long road Hispanic woman must still travel to get to their destination. Hispanic women are getting to their destination without the traditional support most white males have received throughout their career. No wonder most women give up and decide to seek an alternate route to a different more reachable destination. Most Hispanic women have realized how exhausting this road has been and when they reach it they realize it was not worth the effort because after all the struggle and effort it took to get there, they have become a different person. This change that happens often may lead to something better because they have become more confident and knowledgeable about the type of environment they are seeking in their professional growth.

Job satisfaction is something that is very important to many people. Job satisfaction is a pleasurable or positive emotional state resulting from the appraisal of one's job or job experiences (Michel, 1992). A variety of factors that influence an employee's level of job satisfaction include the level of compensation and benefits, promotion opportunities, working conditions, style of management, and the type of position including tasks involved and the challenges the position creates (Moyes, Shao, & Newsome, 2008). I think these are all important factors but would also add respect. Showing employees respect leads to heightened productivity and creativity. Stress related to incivility results in a multibillion-dollar annual hit to the U.S. economy (Hauser, 2011). Respect is extremely important to today's workforce and specifically to Hispanic women because of the differences that have been happening when it comes to recognition and opportunity. It signifies that an employee is being valued and supported. It also means the company values diversity and is open to new ideas and a new way of doing things. I feel most companies do not place enough emphasis on respect and end up losing talented people and underestimate the cost of rehiring and retraining new employees just because they did not take preventive measures.

Morrison's (1993) research listed top management intervention as the primary reason change could happen concerning diversity in higher leadership positions. Morrison's study also revealed that top management recognized the importance of diversity in leadership positions helped with competition. Morrison's study found the four main reasons organizations undertook workforce diversity initiatives was due to facilitating recruitment, enlarging management pool talent, it is the right thing to do, and enlarging the executive pool talent. Again these are similar to the reasons I listed in an earlier chapter but clearly have not helped enforce the promotion of Hispanic women into higher leadership roles. It is hard to prove how many Hispanic women have been turned down for higher level leadership roles without proving it was not discrimination. Hispanic women do not have similar experience because Hispanic women have not been given same opportunities therefore making it that much harder for them to obtain necessary skills and experience to obtain higher leadership positions. If based on Morrison's research and findings of top level executives seeing the absolute necessity of recognizing the importance of diversity in higher level leadership roles then why does under representation of minority women still exist in today's organizations?

This in some ways is hard to answer because there could be numerous reasons. Could this lack of minority representation in leadership continue to be because of weak or indifferent recruitment practices, lack of institutional procedures for recruiting minorities, lack of commitment to diversity, lack of administrative leadership and training programs, or institutional racism, benign neglect and indifference (Muller, 1996)? If advancing minorities in general to higher level positions is difficult already then how much more difficult is it to provide opportunity to a sublet of that minority group such as the Hispanic woman? Again, why are these barriers still present today despite the recognition that diversity in upper leadership roles is important?

As a huge amount of Baby Boomers are getting ready to retire or contemplate retirement, organizations need to start thinking about who is going to be filling these upper management/ leadership roles. It is somewhat strange that at this moment in time there are many Hispanic women who are waving checkered flags in order to be recognized and be given an opportunity to learn and grow and at the same time organizations realize they need to act and take action yet they are still ignoring an important part of the workforce. I am not sure why the hesitation is happening. Most leadership positions are being held by 50+ year old white men and the opportunity is ripe for Hispanic women to gain access to higher level leadership roles. Especially since these women are obtaining higher education, bilingual, multitaskers, entrepreneurs, and motivated then why would they not be considered ideal candidates?

As I kept writing this book, this is the question that kept arising. The world we live in today is not so black and white anymore. When I take a look around not only in the U.S. but where the problem seems to be more prevalent, multiracial people are more present compared to a person of just one race. I also see that most people in general do not mean to discriminate but somehow end up doing it. Is it a lack of awareness? A lack of faith? A fear of change? Furthermore, females are a larger part of that group but does that mean that as worker shortage such as Baby Boomers get ready to retire mean that opportunities will begin to exist for Hispanic women? If we are to base our answer on the past and what is happening now, the answer would be no because statistics have proven this is not the case. This is not to say that it has been a completely lost case because there have been Hispanic women who have overcome these barriers and are successful in higher leadership roles especially in consumer product and packaged good industries because of their consumer power. Unfortunately, the representation of Hispanic women is not as clearly even across other industries compared to other groups. Again I highlight the importance of equal opportunity compared to other groups. Most of my research has found that if Hispanic women want to crack this so called glass ceiling we must be the absolute best and must not bother wasting our time with companies that do not want to invest in us. Otherwise, if you have invested a lot of time and commitment then stay and fight. Does this sound fair? I do not believe so. Why must Hispanic women have to prove themselves any differently?

The impact Hispanic women have faced in seeking higher leadership roles has been hard. Similar to other minorities groups, they have had their fair share of overcoming obstacles. Hispanic women have taken the proper steps such as continuing to support and care for their families, raising children and in many cases raising them as a single parent, pursued and education, and maintained full-time employment. In the workforce, the steps have not been so clear or linear. Obtaining entry level positions has not been difficult but it is only when they have sought higher leadership positions has the obstacles been encountered. In some organizations, efforts are sometimes made and occasional promotions are made but not at the rate it should be that would result in significant amounts of change. As a result, women have had to seek alternate solutions in order to gain experience or seek recognition and value. A significant amount of Hispanic women have found the answer in starting their own businesses. Many have gone on to be successful self entrepreneurs. They have stated it is because as their own bosses they are ultimately responsible for their decisions and outcomes. It provides them with a sense of satisfaction that they have risen up to the challenge and at same been able to balance any issue they may have had with taking care of their families.

Also, by denying Hispanic women access to higher leadership positions, women have gone on to start their own businesses. As more women become entrepreneurs they have helped create another route to reach leadership positions. The exposure they gain as entrepreneurs provides them the necessary management and leadership experience. Since Hispanic women are learning the ropes on their own, they end up practicing, learning, and doing business in a completely different manner than the traditional way the Caucasian male has conducted business. These differences result in creative solutions and outcomes because they have not followed the norm. Because they have also walked a different path in life, the way they handle situations may also not be the same. Their ways may be less rigid and formal because of the lack of mentoring or familiarity with the way things are usually conducted. This may result in their solutions having a fresh and unique outcome. The bonus is that as entrepreneurs their business now benefits whereas if they had remained with their former job such creativity and positive outcomes may not have come to be because of the lack of exposure and mentoring. By learning and being on their own, women have discovered a different leadership style. Some of these leadership differences have included empathy, tolerance, accepting differences, creativity, encouragement, providing praise, acknowledging talent, and better preparedness. Most of these things developed because they were lacking in their interaction from their own professional relationship with their leaders who tended to be male. This is not about which leadership style is better (men or women's) but when dealing with a workforce that is quickly becoming more female Hispanic dominant then it becomes more crucial to have representation.

I think that the major impact for Hispanic women has been on recognizing their own potential and putting a stop to stereotyping. Hispanic women have done this through a variety of methods. They are making sure they do not make the same mistake of not acknowledging differences but instead supporting and nurturing their staff and coworkers. Most of us do not want our own children, especially daughters, to face the same biases and barriers when they are seeking professional opportunities as they get older. Hispanic women want the stereotyping to stop so they have made tremendous strides at stopping these views. They have pursued their education, gained work experience, maintained traditional values, and ventured out and began their own businesses. According to U.S. labor workforce, Hispanic women are not only outpacing other minority women such as African American and Asian but also Hispanic men when it comes to starting up their own businesses.

While facing battles in the workforce, Hispanic women have had to also face battles at home which have been another impact for them while seeking higher leadership roles. Over the years, Hispanic women have slowly become the breadwinners and their families have come to depend on them for their livelihood. They have also had to step out of their traditional roles of obedient daughters and wives to pursue a professional career. While Hispanic women have understood their need to gain higher professional roles their families may not completely understand and support. It can be draining for women to have to battle for what they believe in both at home and work. For many Hispanic women it is a battle they feel is worth fighting because of the investment they have put in getting somewhere in life. I wonder if it is due to the fact that because Hispanic women have always had limitations placed on them that at this time in their lives they are now facing a challenge that is worth overcoming.

They believe in themselves when others do not appear to believe in them most especially in the workforce. This takes a lot of confidence and courage. I know that for me it has been a tough battle and that there were many times when I even doubted myself. I did not like this feeling. If I did not believe in myself then why would I think others could believe in me?

As I turned 40 and my confidence became stronger based on experience and knowledge, things began to become clearer for me. I realized what was most important to me and if my job did not want to put the time and effort to help me in my professional growth then it was their loss not mine. I made a lot of mistakes in my professional career but I would have made a whole lot less if I had the support and encouragement a lot of my male Caucasian co-workers received. I believe that if I had had mentors at higher levels of leadership I would have had been exposed to more opportunities. Males tend to have exposure to mentors that are in more senior level positions which tend to give them the necessary experience that eventually leads to higher leadership positions. I had to do things blindly and to the best of my ability. In the process, I learned and grew. I learned to believe in myself and also gain experience on how to handle future situations differently. I was often told that I came across as passionate (which subtly meant angry) about how I handled situations. It is interesting that Hispanic women are often associated with "passionate". "Sylvia, I admire your passion for your job." "Sylvia, it is clear you are passionate about your beliefs." "Sylvia you passionately demonstrated how you feel." Then in my reviews I would basically be told to be less "passionate" or in other words, be less angry. I still chuckle over these feedbacks I received over the years because these reviewers were afraid to call a spade a spade. Of course, I was passionate about my job. I did not think this was a bad thing. I always thought that when you evoke emotion it means you care. I cared about my job and what I did to make a difference. Part of my reason for writing this book is to share some of the lessons I have learned so that the path to higher leadership positions for other

Hispanic women can be a little less intimidating. I think it is important that not only should we have mentors we can seek or have but also to act as mentors in return.

This past year, I have been watching an interesting show called "Undercover Boss." The show has been fascinating to me because purposely or unpurposly the show reveals a lot about corporate America. This is a show where a chief executive officer goes undercover and finds out how his company is being handled by entry/middle level management and to hopefully find ways in which the company can improve. Along the way, he ends up meeting individuals who end up impacting the CEO. After he meets these individuals, he has a meeting with his senior level executives and gives them a lowdown on his findings. He then meets with these entry/middle management individuals and reveals his true identity. These individuals are then given back feedback and/or acknowledgment for the work they have done for the company. The two points I have found fascinating have been when the CEO meets with his senior level executives. A great majority have been Caucasian men who chuckle and smile and congratulate their boss on a job well done. Second, and there has not been one episode where my eyes do not get misty is when the CEO acknowledges the importance of valuing an employee. It strikes me interesting that this is shocking news to the CEO. Do they forget or is it that many never faced this issue as an individual in the workforce? I look at the CEO making this acknowledgment on national television and their face is in actual awe as if they never had to face this fact before. Is this for real? Could people in upper level management positions be in denial? I have watched four straight episodes this season alone and each of these CEO's has acknowledged the importance of valuing employees and giving them recognition. These CEO's also have provided single mothers with an extra acknowledgment of either advancing their careers by being their mentors or giving them a paid vacation which allows the employee to spend more time with their children. Some of these CEOs have mentioned that it reminds them of their own mothers and the sacrifices their mothers made to raise them and make sure they had ample opportunity. I have sat their and watched and listened to their comments and wondered where in the process of their professional career did they forget what their mothers taught them? Is this forgetfulness on purpose or do they concentrate on issues they feel as having more importance? It could also be that along the way they ended up working with other people who were similar to them so they were not as exposed to the makeup of the current workforce.

I suppose in some ways we will not know the answer as to why not much change has happened concerning diversity. If businesses were to admit and be frank that they have not made much progress would not be good for business. Businesses continue to put other things ahead in their long term strategic planning and diversity just does not often top the list of priorities. Yet, it is so strange that in this era such neglect continues to exist. It is hard to prove but it happens and there is data to show how strongly it is present in our workforce. It may not have been strange to expect 20 to 30 years ago but that it is happening in the 21st century is absurd. Attending high school, college, graduate school, and working has exposed people to all dimensions of life the last 20 years. Realistically, it will take another 10 to 15 years before the workforce will see any difference in upper leadership positions. It will take that much longer for all people to stop looking at people's ethnicity to realize their value. This is most especially true because of the involvement of a worldwide market. People in higher level leadership positions need to have the ability to recognize the creative ability of a diverse workforce and be open to change in order to capitalize on globalization. Ultimately, this is the main reason Hispanic women value on working for a company that places importance on workplace diversity. Hispanic women will then begin to place trust and commitment to a company that believes in them and is going to provide trust and effort in their internal growth.

As the workforce begins to get smaller and more diversified, companies will need to rethink on how to promote and support minority women into higher leadership positions. Some of these companies will look at initiating or improving their mentoring programs and others will acknowledge the importance of valuing their employees at a newer level. Maybe some companies will do both. The bottom line is that companies need to take action now and react to the workforce that is present before them. These individuals are Hispanic women. If these companies end up waiting too long they will end up losing not only a competitive edge but losing these very same workers.

This is because Hispanic women know their capabilities and have a desire to learn and be more. They are seeking companies who are willing to provide opportunities and growth. Recent data reveals the lack of support and guidance Hispanic women are not receiving despite changing demographics in the workforce. What is it going to take for companies to recognize change needs to happen?

Chapter 5

Future Implications for the Hispanic Woman in the Workplace

So here we are today, the Hispanic woman in the workforce. It is a specific workforce that has been steadily growing in number and is going to continue to grow. Hispanic women have faced challenges similar to other minority groups but face greater challenges in fighting against discrimination and upward professional mobility because of the expectations that are placed on them both at home and work and the lack of exposure and support they do not receive in their professional careers. Despite these challenges, Hispanic women are making great strides in raising families by themselves, pursuing and obtaining their education, and seeking professional career advancements with organizations that support their growth. They are also being recognized as a powerful and significant consumer group. Hispanic women no longer have to fear backlash from their families, religious beliefs, personal responsibilities, or professional growth because they have become secure and confident in whom they are and are aiming to become in their lives. They recognize their value and how much they are able to contribute to the world. The changes that have happened in the last few decades has also created opportunities for Hispanic women to be more vocal, independent, and assertive so that they have been able to seek higher education, work experience, and freedom to pursue professional careers in the business world. What makes them different from other groups who faced similar barriers or challenges is that they are making a choice on whether they will remain with organizations that do not recognize their value or move on because they place a greater value on their personal lives and goals. They have reached a point in their lives where they can make choices without feeling as if they have failed.

This is the beauty of living in this present time for Hispanic women. They have choices and no one can force them to do anything they choose not to do or make them unhappy. Many Hispanic women have proven this by moving on and creating their own businesses. They still faced challenges but they have discovered they like being in charge because their past experiences have given them the skills to handle difficult situations. Experiencing these challenges has significance because they own their companies so the decisions they make becomes critical to their success. Hispanic women have faced these challenges in the past so they can relate and react on how to best handle. Often in these cases because of the flexibility of time management, starting their own businesses became the best solution. The flexibility provides the Hispanic women with the ability to raise their children so that they can be an active parent but in other cases provide them with an opportunity to go back and pursue a higher degree. I would like to say we are in a Latina era. We have the whole package of multitasking home, religious, professional, educational beliefs and experiences and paving the future for any new group that should and will emerge in the workforce.

This is important information for companies to understand because of the challenges being faced in the workplace today both domestically and globally. Companies need to recognize the value of such an important workforce and not just by having them in entry level positions or attempting to create diversity programs that have no real outcomes. The opportunities need to exist equally and fairly but not like it is now. This cannot be an occasion to fill the status quo but an opportunity to make significant changes that acknowledges the changing workforce that exists. Because it is not happening and continued lack of succession planning representing the true workforce has led and is leading many Hispanic women to be exasperated, angry and become fed up. As Hispanic women are showing, they react and take action by making changes that will have positive results in their lives or at least they will strive to make it successful. The Hispanic woman is demonstrating they are not afraid to take the necessary steps to change their professional outcome. Does the Hispanic woman need to shed her outer layer, get angry for the business world to recognize she has something to say and demonstrate she can handle? In the end, Hispanic women end up seeking a better way of getting ahead and ultimately it costs the company. Hispanic women are not going to waste their time by staying faithful and committed to a company that is not going to value them or give them an opportunity to grow professionally. Those days are gone when staying loyal to a company for a long period of time was sufficient.

Receiving a pat in the back and an appreciation award given for commitment and loyalty is outdated. People today seek stronger and more fulfilling tokens of appreciation. They want personal recognition. They have invested their time, education, and skills into their jobs with the hope that they can be appreciated and recognized for their valuable input. The type of investment they are now given has cost them a lot of money, time, and personal sacrifice. They want to know that in the long run they are going to have a return on their investment in a positive way. One of those ways is to seek professional growth, compensation, and upward mobility within their organization. Most of us do not want to be grouped and given one huge recognition award.

Somewhere along the way, Hispanic women began to realize their value both at home and in the professional world. I know that for me it was rewarding to know that I was making a difference in my profession. By difference I mean that it meant I was able to help someone understand how they could access medical care, help them understand about their medical health coverage, or interpret what their primary care physician was telling them. Eventually, I found it important to help people of all ethnic backgrounds understand how to access primary care services and how to also be financially responsible when seeking these services. At the same time, I learned the importance of an education. I believed or was led to believe that if you had education then it would mean you had a better chance at a promotion. For me a promotion meant exposure to learning new things and opportunities. As the years went by and my work skills improved and by supplementing it with an education then it was going to be smooth sailing all the way to the golden land of opportunities in the professional business world. Of course this was not true and it ended up being a very difficult road to travel because the opportunities did not come so easily. Depending on which stage you are in your life this could end up being a very difficult time in your life where major decisions need to be made concerning your professional career. The decision you make has to also balance out with your personal responsibilities which makes the whole decision making process more difficult and heart wrenching. I know that for me I loved learning and gaining a better perspective on the delivery and access of healthcare to our community and knowing I was making a difference. I then would go home, switch roles, and take over the household duties but at same time keep that managerial role which came in handy when making decisions and setting rules at home. Furthermore, it benefited me in school because I could relate to the course work based on my actual work scenarios and gain a better perspective on what I was learning. The whole idea of making a difference was very important to me during this period of my life. I now realize that making a difference is still important to me but it has to be me who places the most value and recognition in it and not anyone else.

I am not sure if this is due to our religious faiths or the way we were raised by our parents or that we are at a perfect time to take action so that we can discover professional satisfaction also. Is this due because we are a group that places a tremendous amount of belief on tradition or are we creatures of habit? On the other hand, is it something that when it comes to our professional careers we have no qualm about breaking out of the norm now? This norm that we are fighting is discrimination and the fact that we are not able to have equal opportunity at being able to obtain higher leadership positions.

Looking back on my own life as a Hispanic woman, I can see why I am not afraid to ask for more when it specifically concerns my professional career. I have been placed with a tremendous amount of responsibility since I was a young girl and I really did not have much room for failure. If I failed I basically was risking the livelihood of people who were very important to me. Both my parents worked jobs where they had to work different shifts in order not to have to rely on daycare. Eventually as we grew older, I became responsible for taking care of my brothers while my parents were at work. Taking care of my brothers also included cleaning the house and taking them to their appointments and making sure they went to school. Over time, I also became the person who translated, navigated, bargained, shopped, and helped manage household affairs. This all happened when I was between the ages of 9 and 17 years old. By the time I was 17, my father had passed away and my brothers were teenagers who were getting into trouble so I remember these years as constantly visiting the principal or waiting for my brothers after school while they served detention. Back then you could act as a substitute for the parent and because my mother had a job that was not flexible as far as letting her have time off to handle family matters, I was the ideal candidate who needed to handle matters at home.

By the time I started my own family I had plenty of experience on handling family matters despite my young age. Part of this experience helped me be a good parent who did not panic or give in easily. I am not sure if this was also the reason I was able to multitask and handle a lot of responsibility at once. Having had a lot of responsibility at a young age provided me with sensibility and great organization skills that really came in handy. At the time this may not have been so clear and easy to understand but upon reflection it was extremely critical and I believe to this date that I have been very lucky and fortunate to have gone through this experience.

The stuff I have experienced throughout my life has helped me be good at balancing my personal and professional life. It has not been easy at all but I have always loved a challenge. Most especially during those years when my children were little and my personal life was a mess I felt I was going to go crazy but I held on and am now just beginning to appreciate all I have learned along the way. My learning experience has gained me so much insight with my personal and professional life and like other Hispanic women strongly feel has provided me with an advantage. The advantage is the ability to understand and be able to lead change with today's diverse workforce. Organizations should realize the importance of being ready to align business strategies with such a group in leadership positions in order to better achieve growth, profitability, and sustainability. Besides the profitability and marketability advantage it is in company's best interest and to attain good public relations to stop ignoring the fact that there is not enough minorities in their higher leadership positions. Companies must start taking some type of action that shows they understand the importance of change that reflects reality and it also proves that the company respects individuals regardless of their race, ethnicity, beliefs, etc. In general, the lack of minority women such as Hispanic women in top leadership positions in the majority of companies could provide a competitive advantage if they were to act quickly. Sooner rather than later, companies will have to have Hispanic women representation in their leadership positions.

Some organizations like Procter & Gamble spend millions of dollars contributing to education such as the Hispanic

Scholarship Program and the United Negro College Fund in order to help support the education, hiring, retention, and advancement of minorities into their chosen fields. The fact still remains that companies are still lagging with hiring minority females into leadership positions despite all the reasons and proof that this does not make good business sense. Is the refusal to make such leadership changes more important than the survival of a company? Why is there any effort still being placed on not changing an organization's leadership format?

The under representation of Hispanic women in higher leadership positions in an organization is a taboo. It is a taboo because no one will admit out loud it still exists. Everyone from human resources to managers will deny it is happening in their company or under their watch. A few decades ago, in the early 80's, this may have been fine because Hispanic women were just beginning to enter the workforce, but as they sought and gained an education and personal experience, they recognized their capabilities and abilities to add value to their work within these organizations. Hispanic women began to realize the importance of a career and the fulfillment it gave them and they liked it for a variety of reasons. Over time, they saw they were not given the same opportunities or support to move ahead at a similar pace as their white, male coworkers. In fact, they saw they were not given any opportunities or encouragement at growth compared to any other group in the company.

The number of minority women in the workforce, especially Hispanic women, is going to continue to increase. Women are going to be the better part of the workforce compared to men. Unlike past history, women are not going to relinquish their responsibilities at home. They will continue to carry the burden of managing and balancing home/work responsibilities. Hispanic women will not put aside the beliefs they have grown up with and cast them aside because of their professions but will seek companies who are going to support them. As these companies go through transformations and begin to see and accept a changing workforce, these companies will need to start to change the way they view employee expectations. Companies are going to have to change their practices in order to hold on to valuable employees who are contributing to the company's growth. I think it will become easier as more of these companies have leadership that accepts and recognizes the changes that are happening. Most likely this acceptance will happen when that leadership consists of people who have traveled down similar roads like the Hispanic woman.

I have mentioned the importance for companies to recognize the emergence of the Hispanic woman in the workforce and their rapid growth. I have also defined this group as a minority one. The word minority itself implies negativity because it appears that we are referring to something that is inferior and subject to differential treatment. John N. Doggett (2001) commented "I'm not a minority; I'm an American. I am not a victim; I'm a victor." He stated there is nothing positive about the word minority. He stated it means the same thing which means you have no power and because of that he will not allow anyone to call him a minority. This was brought to my attention by a friend of mine who vehemently stated he disliked the word minority. He said, "I pay my taxes and I work hard. I am not a minority." When he stated this it hit me that he was correct. Hispanic women are not minorities. It is offensive and it does imply prejudice. Since times have changed and the number of

Hispanic women has grown in size, it is an outdated word to use with this particular group and one in which implies more as underprivileged or disadvantaged.

The Hispanic woman in today's workforce has moved from being a minority part of the workforce into the majority part of the workforce. Their experience, skills, education, and capabilities have made them a valuable group that is strongly needed in the business world. The ability to help support and guide Hispanic women so that they can have equal opportunities at higher leadership positions needs to be in place now. Organizations are placing themselves at a disadvantage if they do not take advantage at the opportunity of learning from this unique workforce. Hispanic women represent a realistic picture of today's workforce which is people who place a high priority on their family coming first and work second. They are focused, committed individuals who have clear goals regarding their professional careers but continue to remain true to their beliefs and family values. The Hispanic woman seeks equal opportunities at learning and moving up the executive leadership ladder regardless of their race and gender.

The time has come for businesses and organizations to make changes in how they are viewing their workforce. Businesses and organizations need to replace their current internal pipeline development methods (if they have any) so that it includes Hispanic women. They need to initiate or strengthen their mentoring programs so that there are opportunities at seeking out talented individuals who could eventually contribute to the company's success in the future. Without some of these changes Hispanic women will continue to be under-represented in senior leadership roles.

Bibliography

Agocs, C., & Burr, C. (1996). Employment equity, affirmative action and managing diversity: Assessing the differences. *International Journal of Manpower, 17,* 4/5, 30-46.

Allen, R.S., & Montgomery, K.A. (2001). Applying an organizational development approach to creating diversity. *Organizational Dynamics, 30,* 2, 149-161.

Athey, S., Avery, C., & Zemsky, P. (2000). Mentoring and diversity. *American Economic Review, 90,* 4, 765-786.

Behnke, A.O., Piercy, K.W., & Diversi, M. (2004). Educational and occupational aspirations of Latino youths and their parents. *Hispanic Journal of Behavioral Sciences, 26,* 16-35.

Bergeron, D.M., Block, C.J., & Echtenkamp, A. (2006). Disabling the able: Stereotype threat and women's work performance. *Human Performance, 19,* 2, 133-158.

Blank, R., & Slipp, S. (1994). The white male: An endangered species? *Management Review, 83,* 9, 27-33.

Cabrera, E. (2009). Fixing the leaky pipeline: Five ways to retain female talent. *People & Strategy, 32,* 1, 40-45.

Catalyst (2005a). *Alliance for board diversity.* Full report on women and minorities on Fortune 100 boards. New York, NY.

Catalyst (2005b). *Catalyst study exposes how gender-based stereotyping sabotages women in the workplace.* New York, NY.

Charan, R., Drotter, S., & Noel, J. (2001). The leadership pipeline. How to build the leadership-powered company. San Francisco, CA: Jossey-Bass, Inc.

Chowdhury, S. (2000). Management 21c. Someday we'll all manage this way. London: Pearson Education Limited.

Clugson, M., Howell, J., & Dorfman, P. (2000). Does cultural socialization predict multiple bases and foci of commitment? *Journal of Management, 26,* 1, 5-30.

Collins, J.C., & Porras, J.I. (1994). Built to last. Successful habits of visionary companies. HarperCollins Publishers, Inc. New York, NY.

Cornelius, N., & Gagnon, S. (2004). Still bearing the mark of Cain? Ethics and inequality measurement. *Business Ethics, 13,* 1, 26-40.

Dev, R. (2009). Gender sensitivity in corporate environment. *Vikapia: The Journal for Decision Makers, 34,* 4, 92-95.

Dreachslin, J.L. (2007). The role of leadership in creating a diversity-sensitive organization. *Journal of Healthcare Management, 52,* 3, 151-155.

Drucker. P.F. (2008). The essential Drucker: The best of sixty years of Peter Drucker's essential writings in management. NY: HarperCollins Publishers, Inc.

Drucker, P.F. (1999). Management challenges for the 21st Century. NY: HarperCollins Publishers, Inc.

Eagly, A.H., Johannesen-Schmidt, M.C., & van Engen, M.L. (2003). Transformational, transactional and laissez-faire leadership styles: A meta-analysis comparing women and men. *Psychological Bulletin, 129,* 569-591.

Eagly, A.H., & Johnson, B.T. (1990). Gender and leadership style: A meta-analysis. *Psychological Bulletin, 108*, 233-256.

Eng, P. (2009). The era of the bridge builder: Identifying the qualities of "fluent leaders". *National Civic Review, 98*, 3, 34-39.

Gathers, D. (2003). Diversity management: An imperative for healthcare organizations. *Hospital Topics, 81*, 3, 14-20.

Gregory, R.F. (2002). Women and workplace discrimination: Overcoming barriers to gender inequality. *Rudgers University Press.*

Hernandez, T.J., & Morales, N.E. (1999). Career, culture, and compromise: Career development experiences of Hispanics working in higher education. *Career Development Quarterly, 48*, 1, 45-58.

Hewitt Associates (n.d.). Preparing for the Workforce of Tomorrow. Retrieved July 26, 2010, from http://www.hewittassociates.com/intl/na/en-us/KnowledgeCenter/ArticlesReports/ArticleDetail.aspx.cid=1734

Hite, L.M. (2007). Hispanic women managers and professionals: Reflections on life and work. *Gender, Work & Organization, 14*, 1, 20-36.

Hollander, E.P., & Yoder, J. (1980). Some issues in comparing women and men as leaders. *Basic & Applied Social Psychology, 1*, 3, 267-280.

Ibarra, J. (2006). Closing the talent management gap. *Strategic HR Review, 5*, 3, 20-23.

Ingham, J. (2006). Closing the talent management gap. *Strategic HR Review, 5*, 3, 20-23. 2004)

Joiner, T.A., Bartram, T., & Garreffa, T. (2004). The effects of mentoring on perceived career success, commitment, and turnover intentions. *Journal of American Academy of Business, Cambridge, 5,* ½, 164-170.

Kamenou, N. (2008). Reconsidering work-life balance debates: Challenging limited understanding of the 'life' component in the context of ethnic minority women's experiences. *British Journal of Management, 1,* 19, S99-S109.

Kirby, E.L., & Harter, L.M. (2003). Speaking the language of the bottom-line: The metaphor of "Managing Diversity". *Journal of Business Communication, 40,* 1, 28-49.

Lantz, P.M. (2008). Gender and leadership in healthcare administration: 21st Century Progress and Challenges. *Journal of Healthcare Management, 53,* 5, 291-301.

Lewis, A.E., & Fergenson, E.A. (1995). Strategies for developing women managers: How well do they fulfill their objectives? *Journal of Management Development, 14,* 2, 39-54.

Magretta, J. (2002). What management is. How it works and why it's everyone's business. NY: The Free Press, Inc.

Mani, B.G. (1997). Gender and the federal senior executive service: Where is the glass ceiling? *Public Personnel Management, 26,* 4, 545-559.

Mannix, E., & Neale, M.A. (2005). What differences make a difference? *Psychological Science in the Public Interest, 6,* 2, 31-55.

Meyerson, D., & Fletcher, J.K. (2000). A modest manifesto for shattering the glass ceiling. *Harvard Business Review, 78,* 1, 126-136.

Michel, A.J. (1992). Goodbyes can cost plenty in Europe. *Fortune, 16.*

Moberg, D.J., & Velasquez, M. (2004). The ethics of mentoring. *Business Ethics Quarterly, 14,* 1, 9-122.

Morrison, A. (1993). Workforce diversity and the glass ceiling: Practices, barriers, possibilities. *Human Resource Planning,* retrieved September 13, 2010 from www.allbusiness.com/legal/laws-government-regulations-employment/417380.html

Morrison, A.M., & Von Glinow, M. (1990). Women and minorities in management. *American Psychologist, 45,* 2, 200-208.

Morrison, A.M., White, R.P., Van Velsor, E., & The Center for Creative Leadership (1987). Breaking the glass ceiling: Can women reach the top of America's largest corporations? Reading, MA: Addison-Wesley.

Moyes, G.D., Shao, L.P., & Newsome, M. (2008). Comparative analysis of employee job satisfaction in the accounting profession. *Journal of Business & Economics Research, 6,* 2, 65-81.

Muller, G.H. (1996). Gateways to success: Urban community colleges and administrative diversity. San Francisco, CA: Jossey-Bass

Ojeda, L., & Flores, L.Y. (2008). The influence of gender, generation level, parents' educational level, and perceived barriers on the educational aspirations of Mexican American high school students. *Career Development Quarterly, 57,* 1, 84-95.

Peters, T.J., & Waterman, R.H. (2001). In search of excellence. NY: HarperCollins Publishers, Inc

Powell, G.N., & Butterfield, D.A. (2002). Exploring the influence of decision maker's race and gender on actual promotions to top management. *Personnel Psychology, 55,* 2, 397-428.

Prime, J.L., Carter, N.M., & Welbourne, T.M. (2009). Women "Take care", Men "Take charge": Managers' stereotypic perceptions of women and men leaders. *Psychiatrist-Manager Journal, 12,* 1, 25-49.

Rhode, D. (2003). Difference "difference" Makes: Women and Leadership. Stanford University Press.

Robinson, G., & Dechant, K. (1997). Building a business case for diversity. *Academy of Management Executive, 11, 3, 21-31.*

Ruderman, M.N., & Ohlo, P.J. (1995). Promotion decisions as a diversity practice. *Journal of Management Development, 14,* 2, 6-24.

Ryan, M.K., & Haslam, S.A. (2007). The glass cliff: Exploring the dynamics surrounding the appointment of women to precarious leadership positions. *Academy of Management Review, 32,* 2, 549-572.

Schuck, K., & Liddle, B.J. (2004). The female manager's experience: A concept map and assessment tool. *Consulting Psychology Journal: Practice & Research, 56,* 2, 75-87.

Sosik, J.J., & Lee, D.L. (2002). Mentoring in organizations: A social judgment perspective for developing tomorrow's leaders. *Journal of Leadership & Organizational Studies, 8,* 17-32.

Thomas, D.A. (2001). The truth about mentoring minorities: Race matters. *Harvard Business Review, 79,* 4, 98-107.

Thomas, D.A. (1990). The impact of race on manager's experiences of developmental relationships (mentoring and sponsorship): An intra-organizational study. *Journal of Organizational Behavior, 11,* 479-492.

Van Vianen, A.E.M., & Fischer, A.H. (2002). Illuminating the glass ceiling: The role of organizational culture preferences. *Journal of Occupational & Organizational Psychology, 75*, 3, 315-337.

Wasburn, M.H., & Crespo, A.W. (2006). Strategic collaboration: Developing a more effective mentoring model. *Review of Business, 27*, 1, 18-25.

Weech-Maldonado, R., Dreachslin, J.L., Dansky, K.H., De Souza, G., & Gatto, M. (2002). Racial/ethnic diversity management and cultural competency: The case of Pennsylvania Hospitals. *Journal of Healthcare Management, 47*, 2, 111-125.

Wellington, S., & Spence, B. (2001). Be your own mentor: Strategies from top women on the secrets of success. *Random House Publishing Group*.

Wentling, R.M. (2004). Factors that assist and barriers that hinder the success of diversity initiatives in multinational corporations. *Human Resource Development International, 7*, 2, 165-180.

Young, A.M. (2000). The exchange relationship between mentors and protégés: The development of a framework. *Human Resource Management Review, 10*, 2, 177-210.

Zahra, S.A. (1999). The changing rules of global competitiveness in the 21st century. *Academy of Management Executive, 13*, 1, 36-42.